Vocabulary of Shapes Coloring Book: Volume One

Copyright © 2021 John Wesley Boccardo

All rights reserved. This book may not be reproduced, in whole or in part, in any form, without written permission by the publisher.

ISBN: 978-1-7370525-1-7

VOCABULARY OF SHAPES

COLORING BOOK ONE

WESLEY BOCCARDO

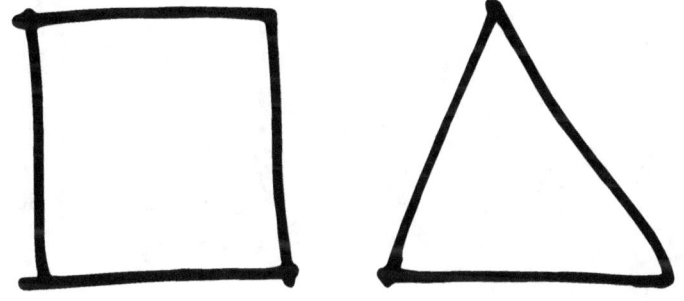

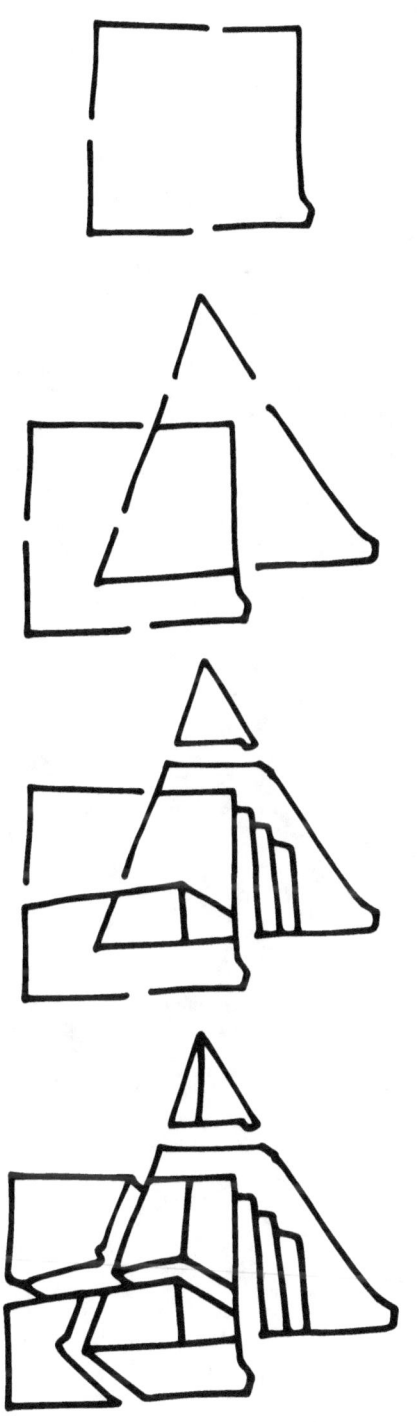

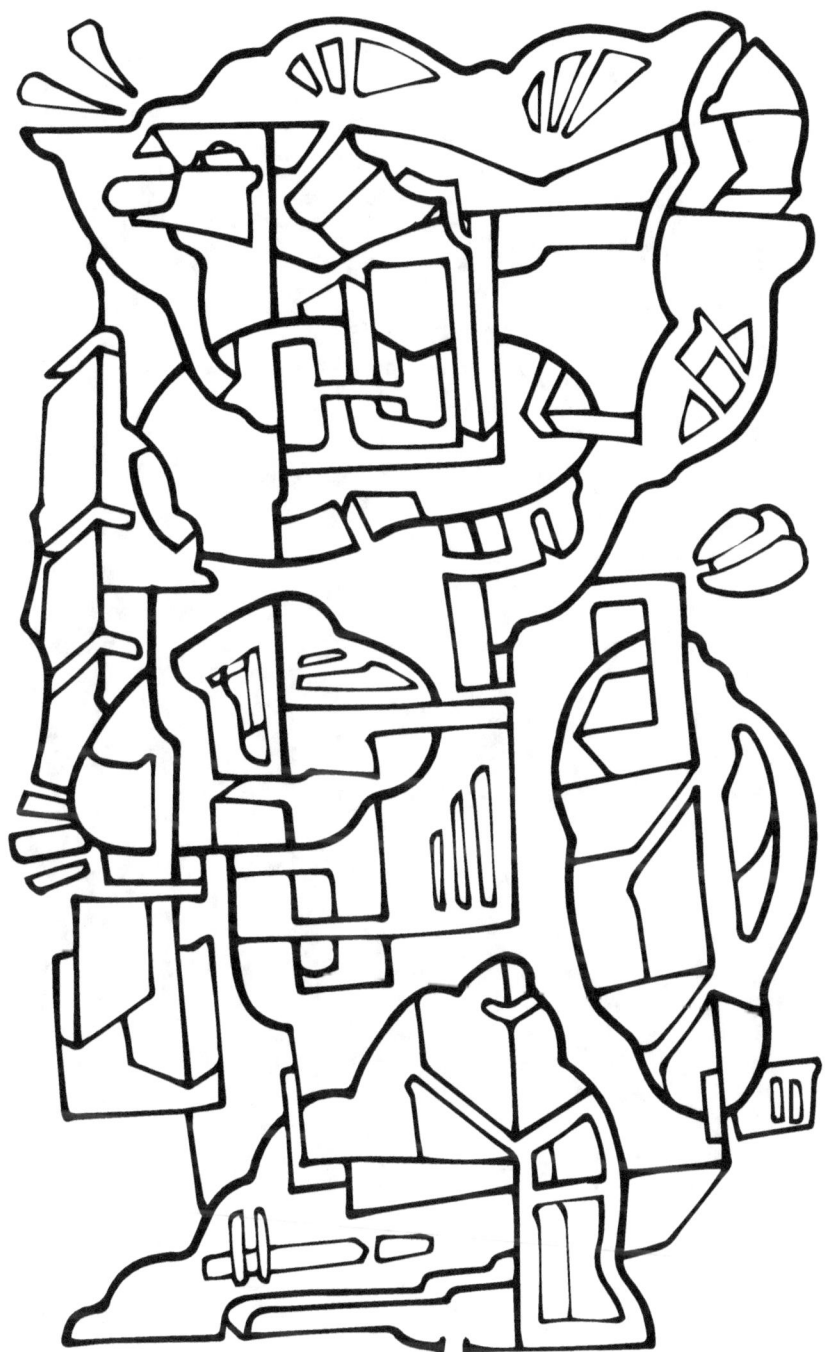

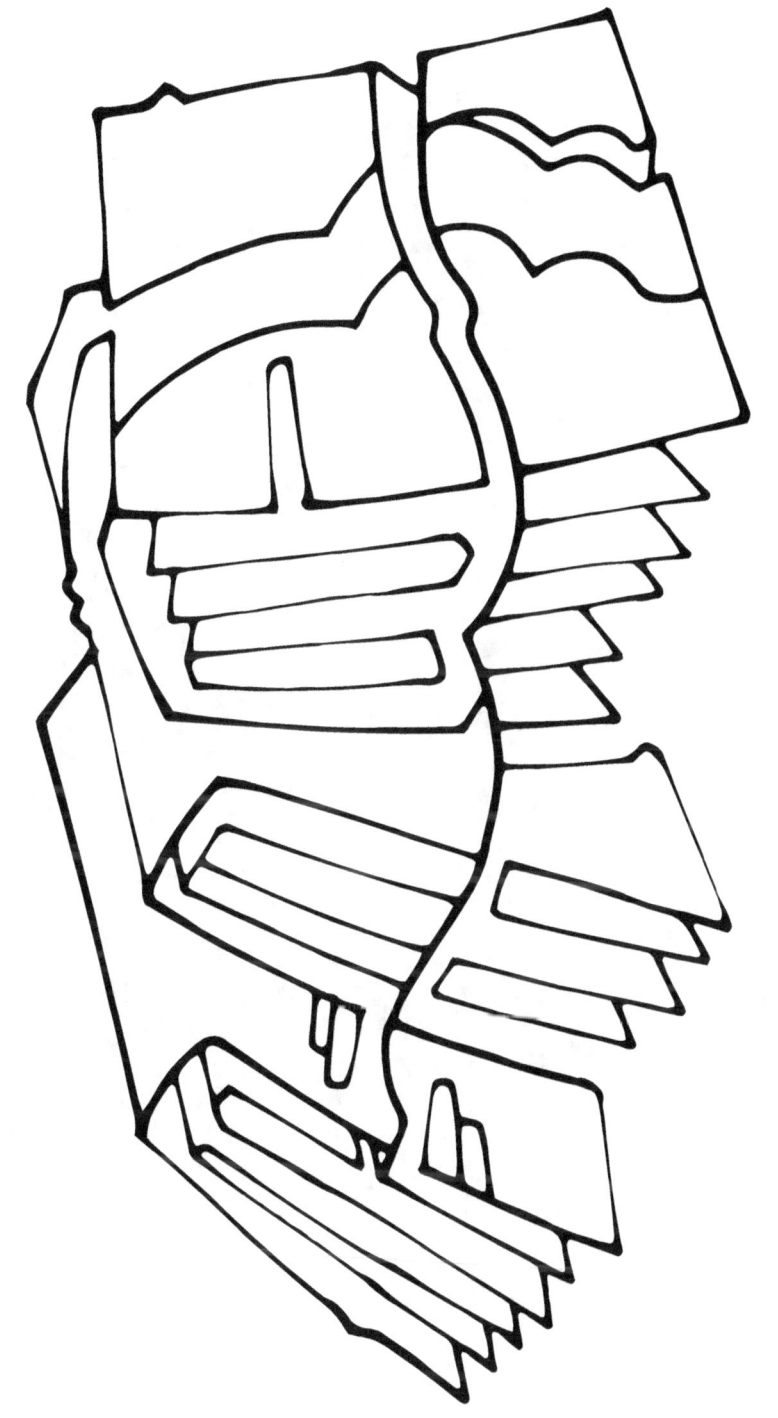

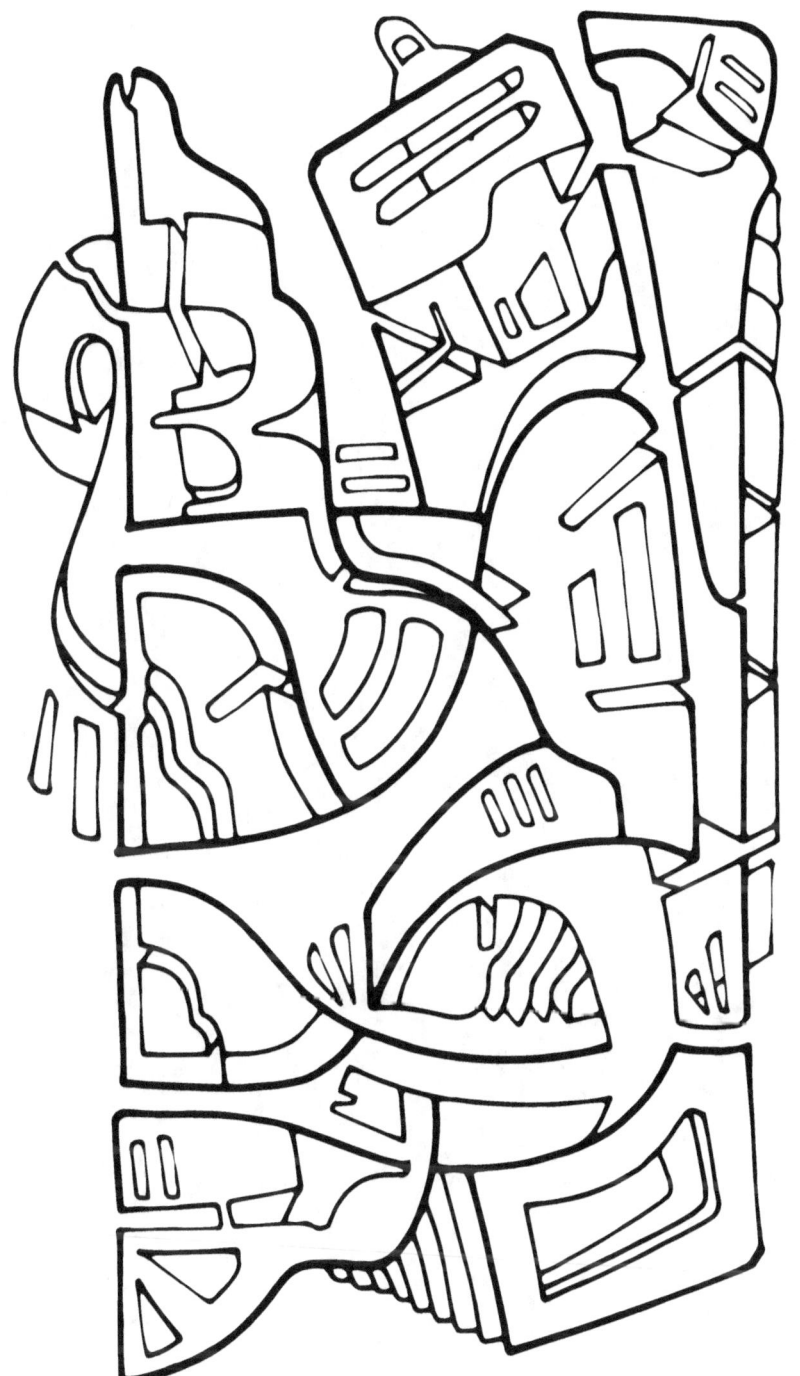

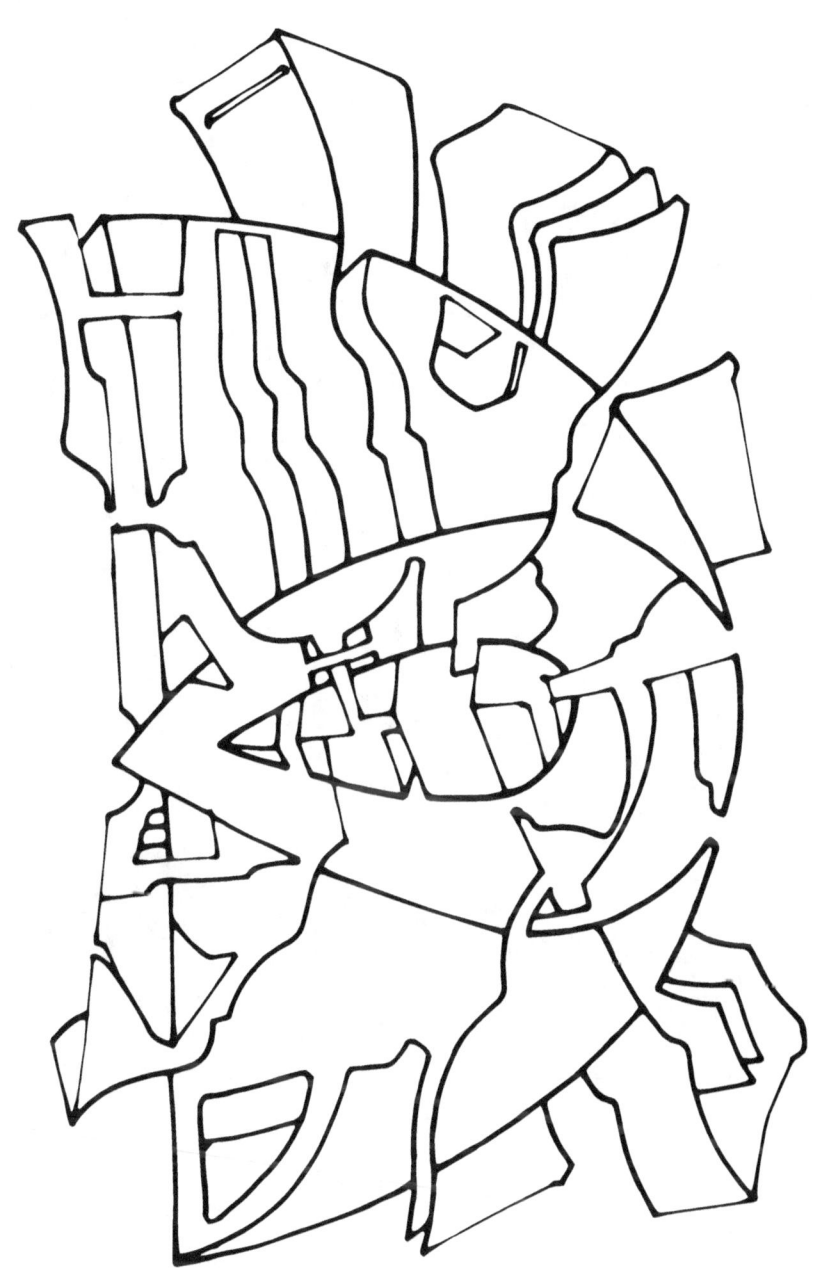

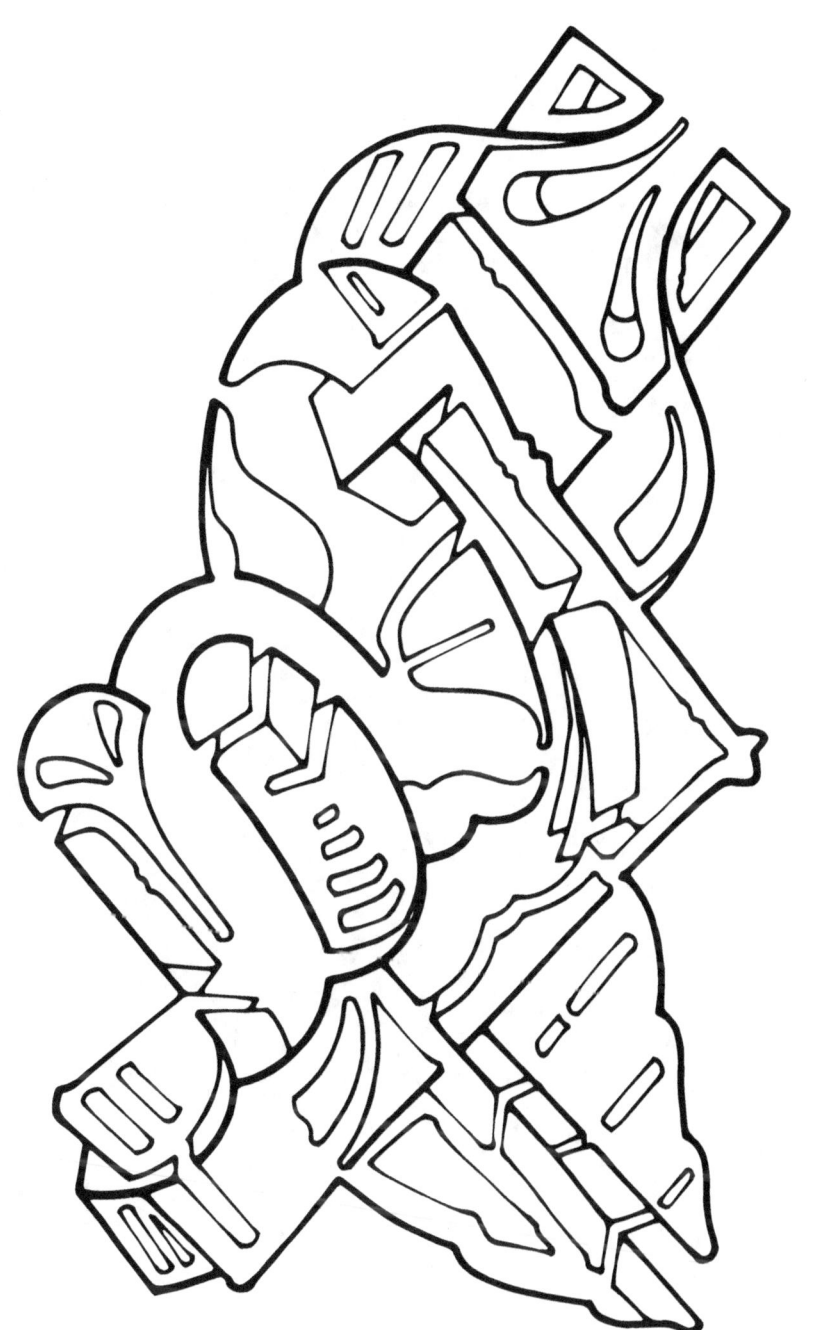

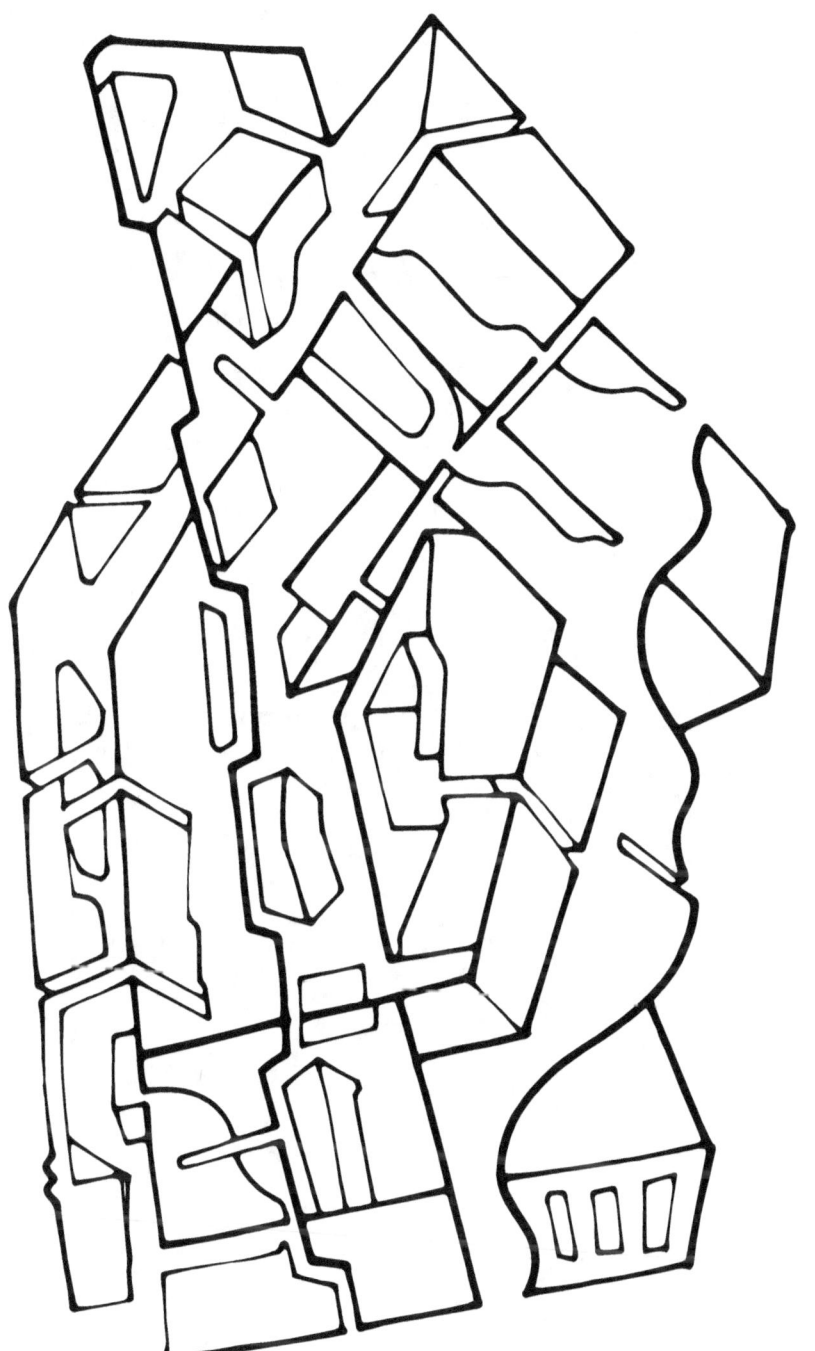

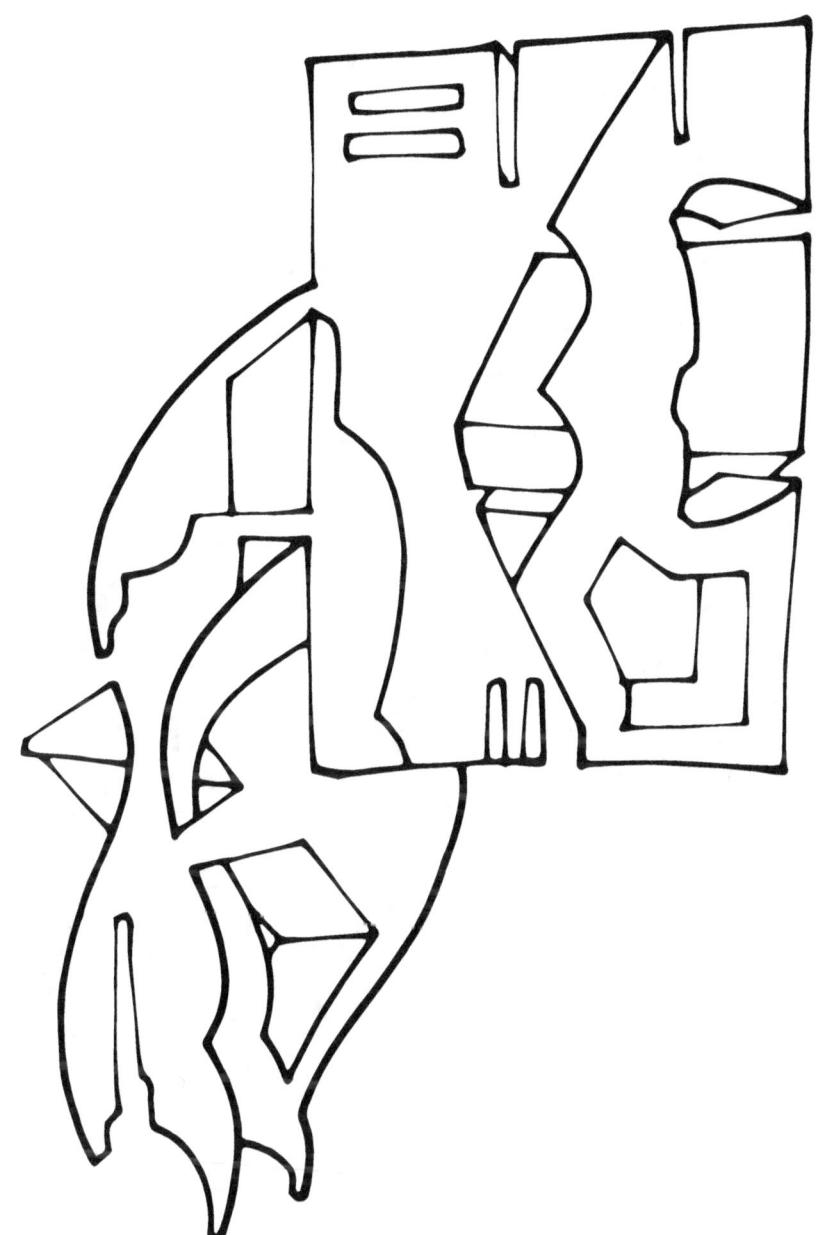

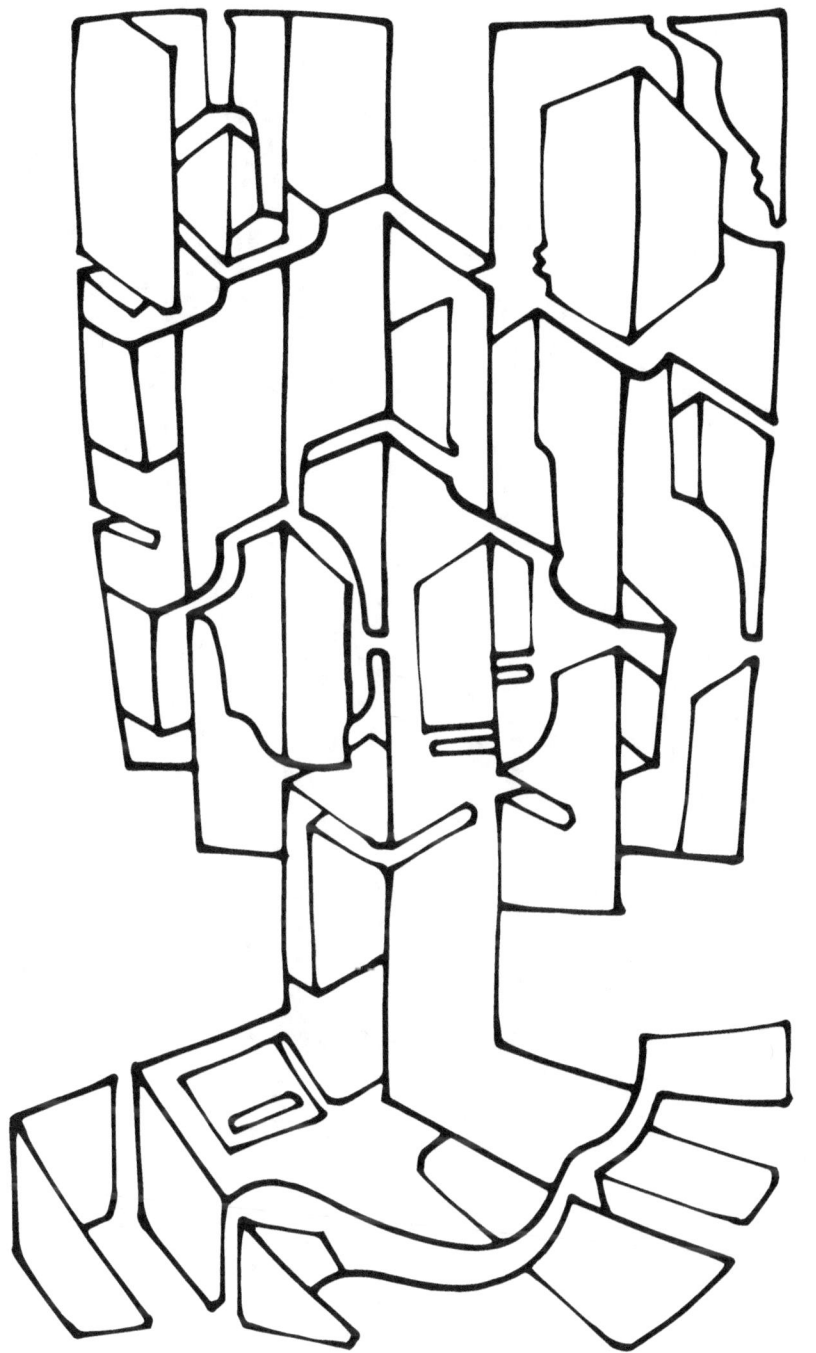

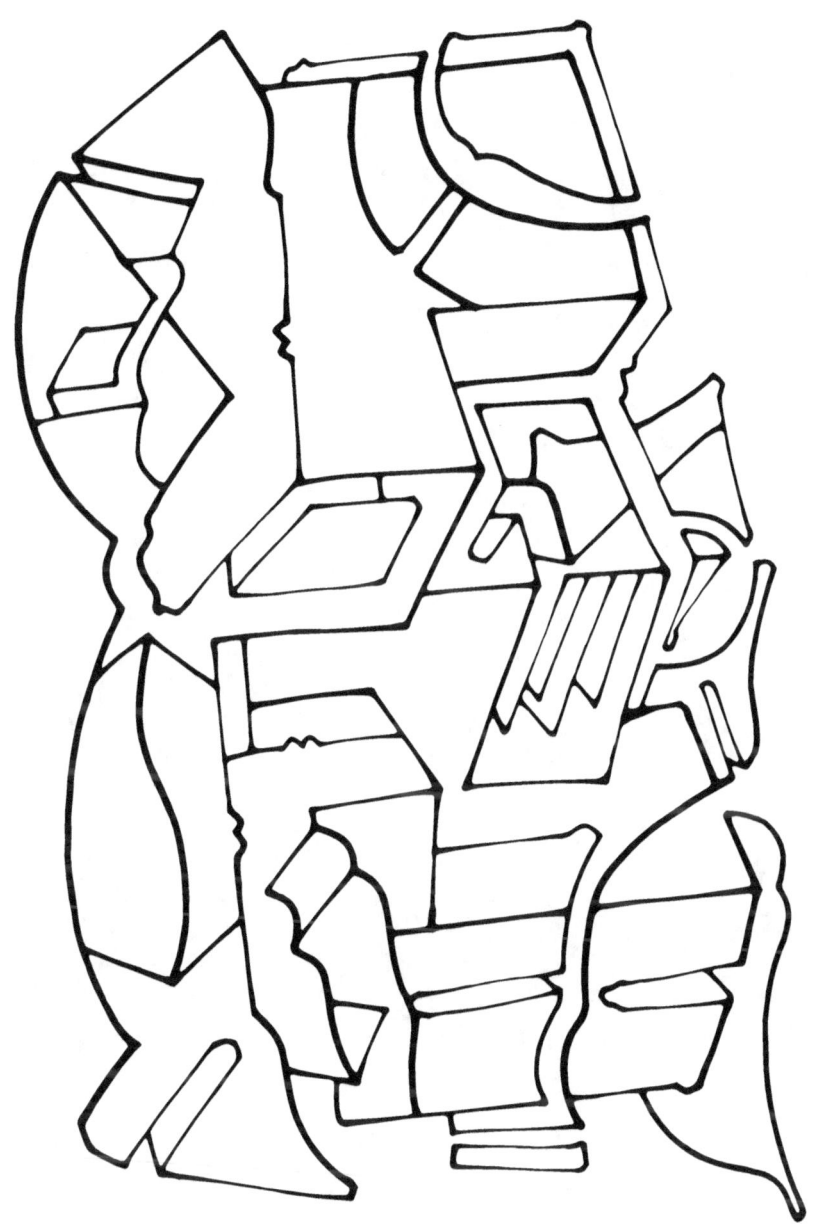

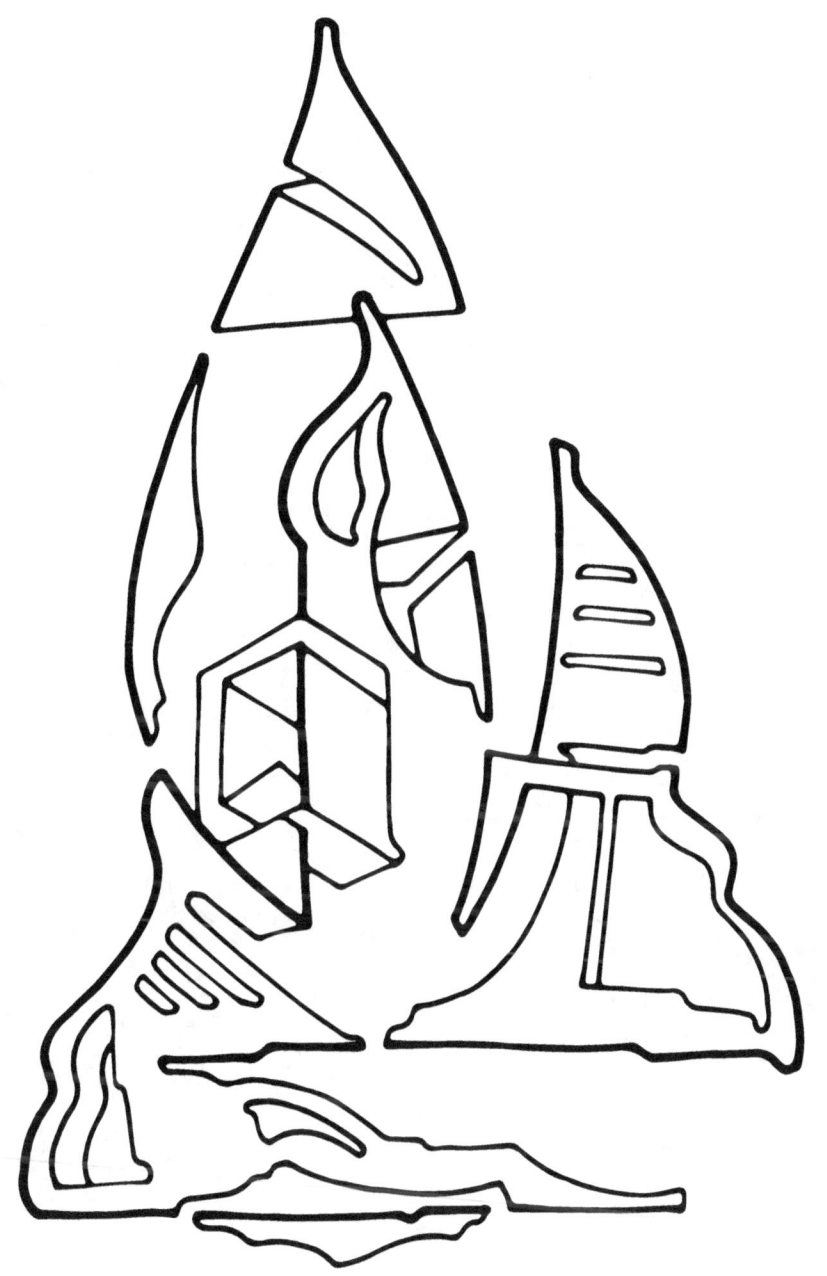

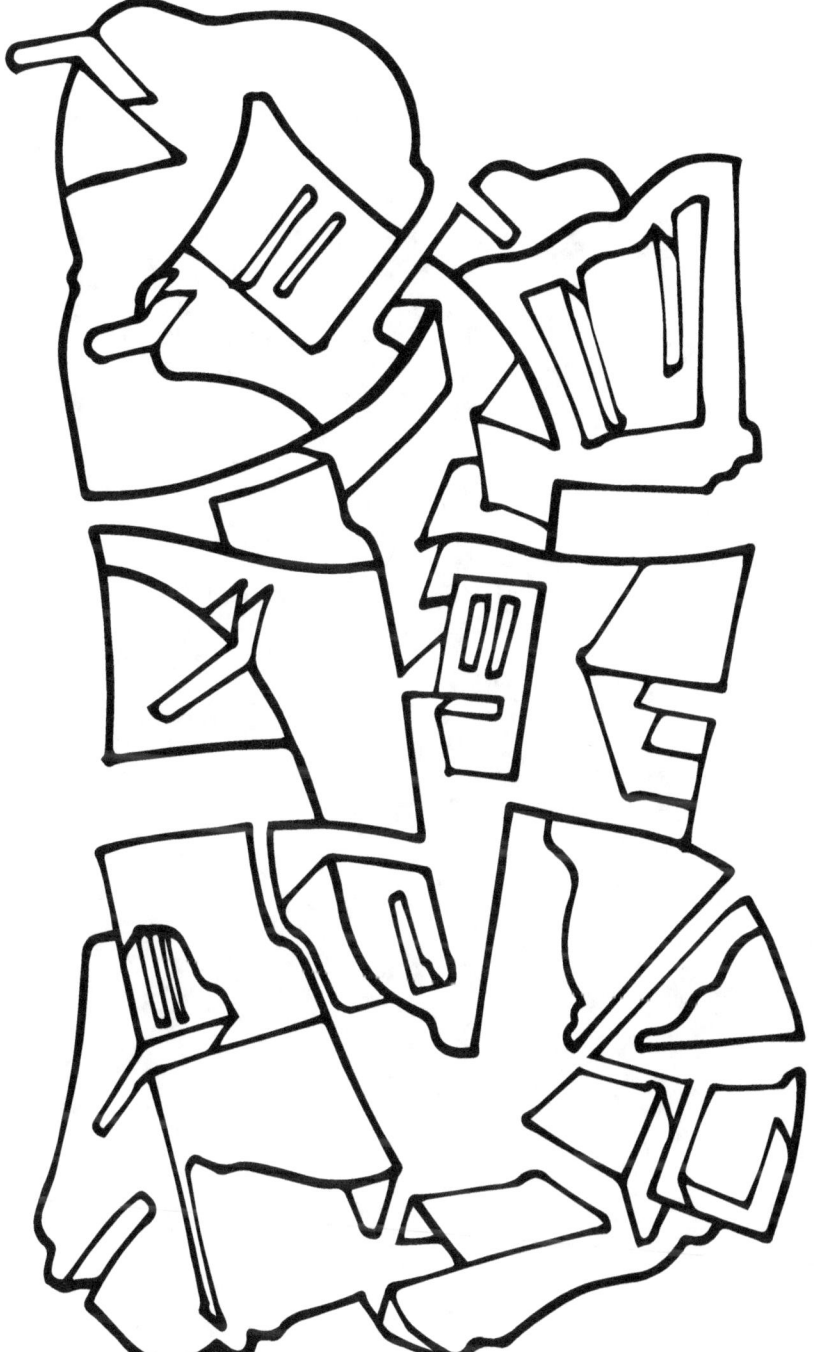

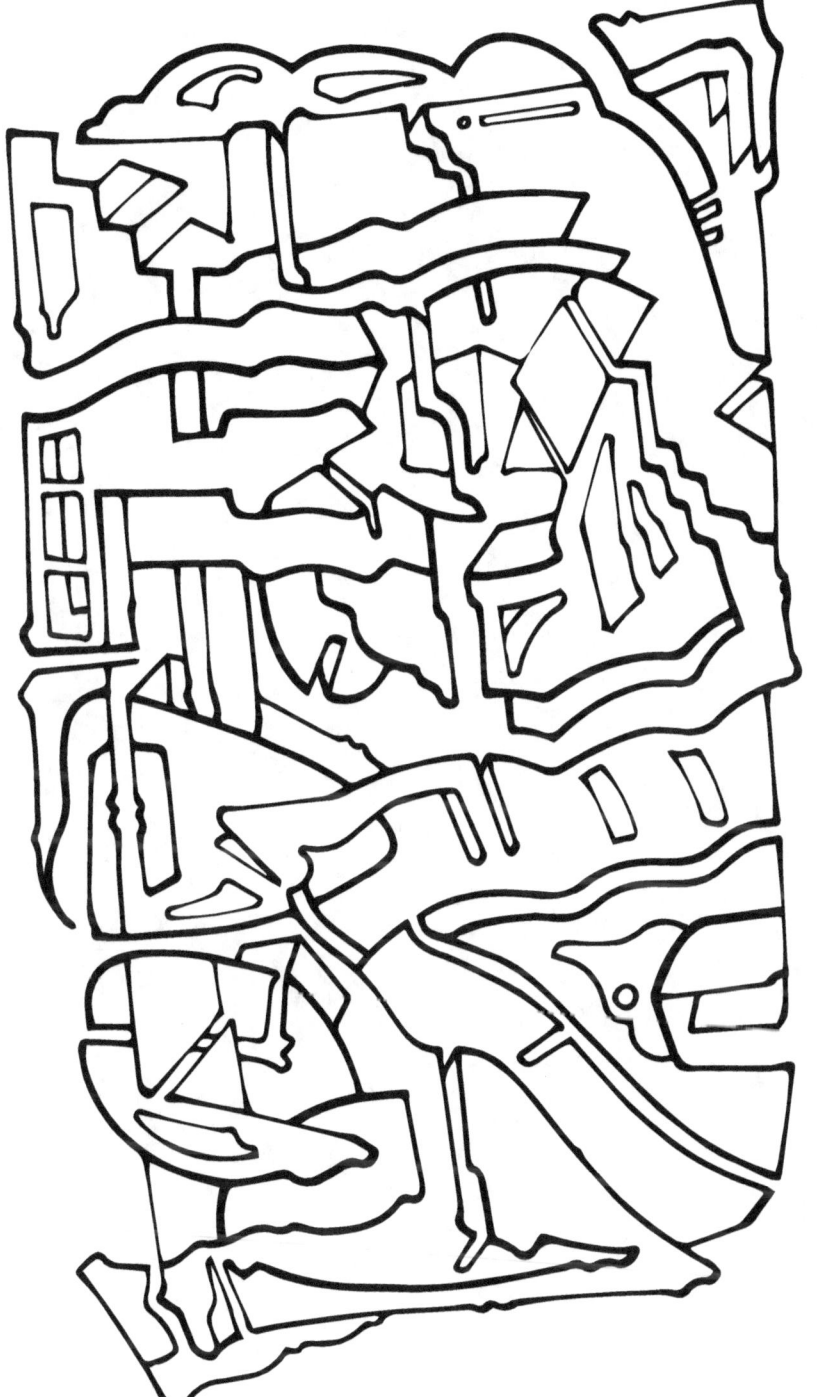

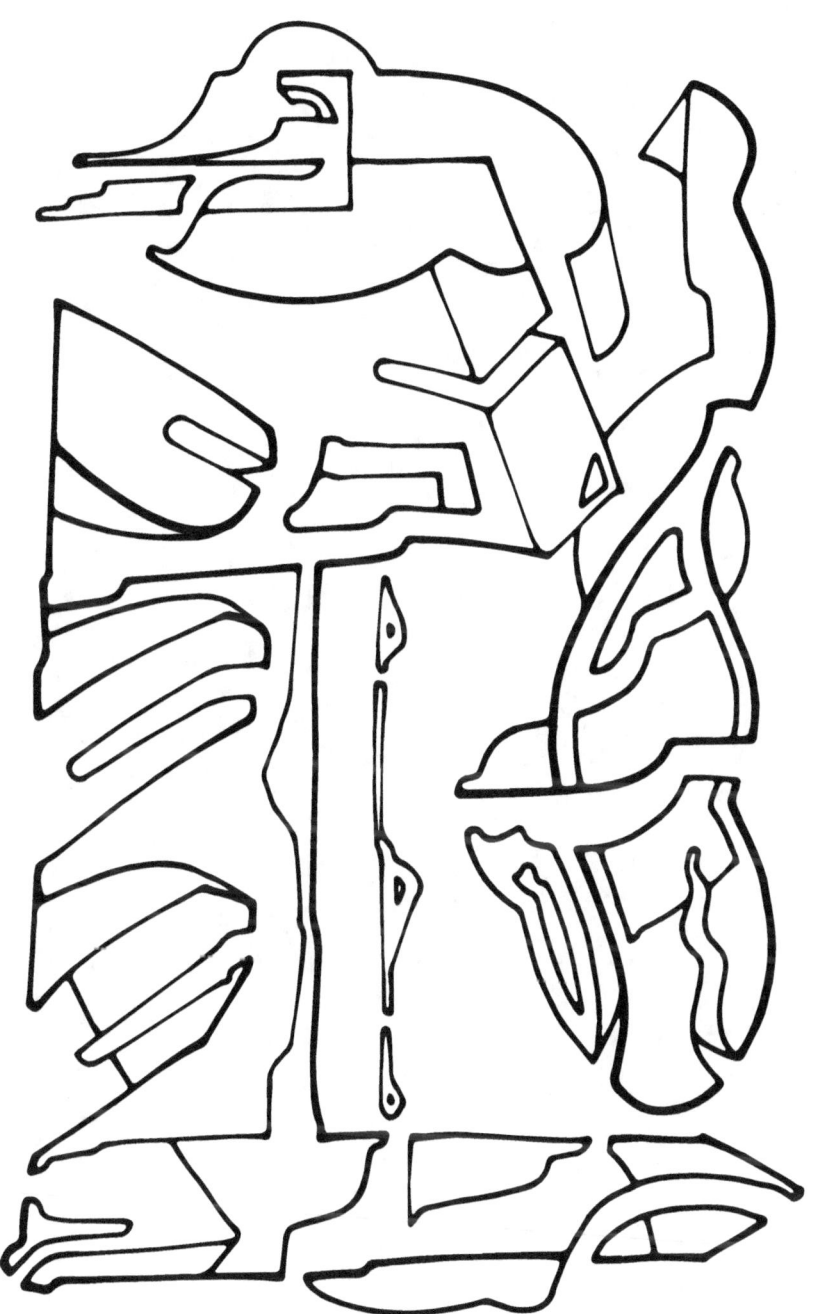

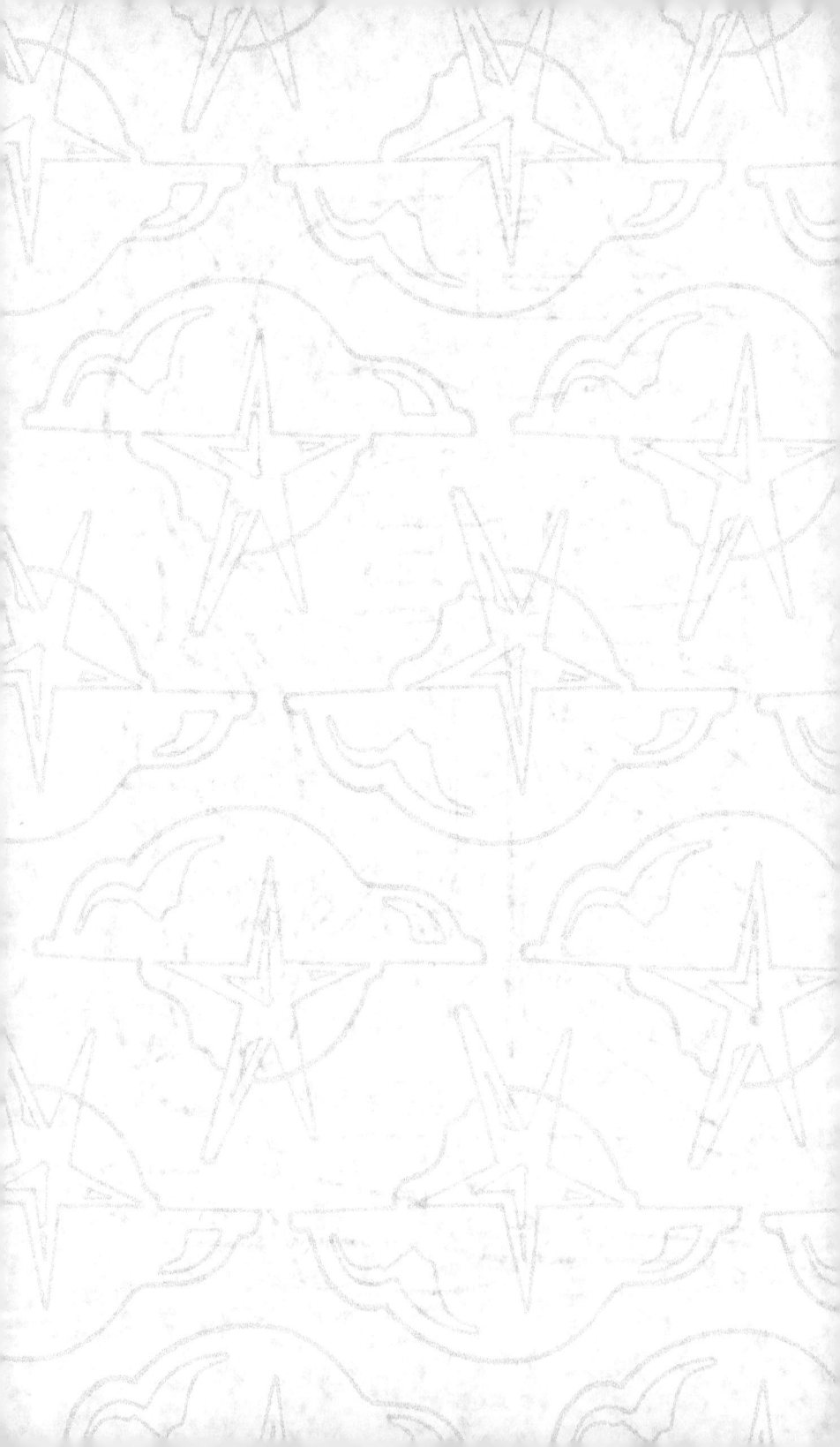

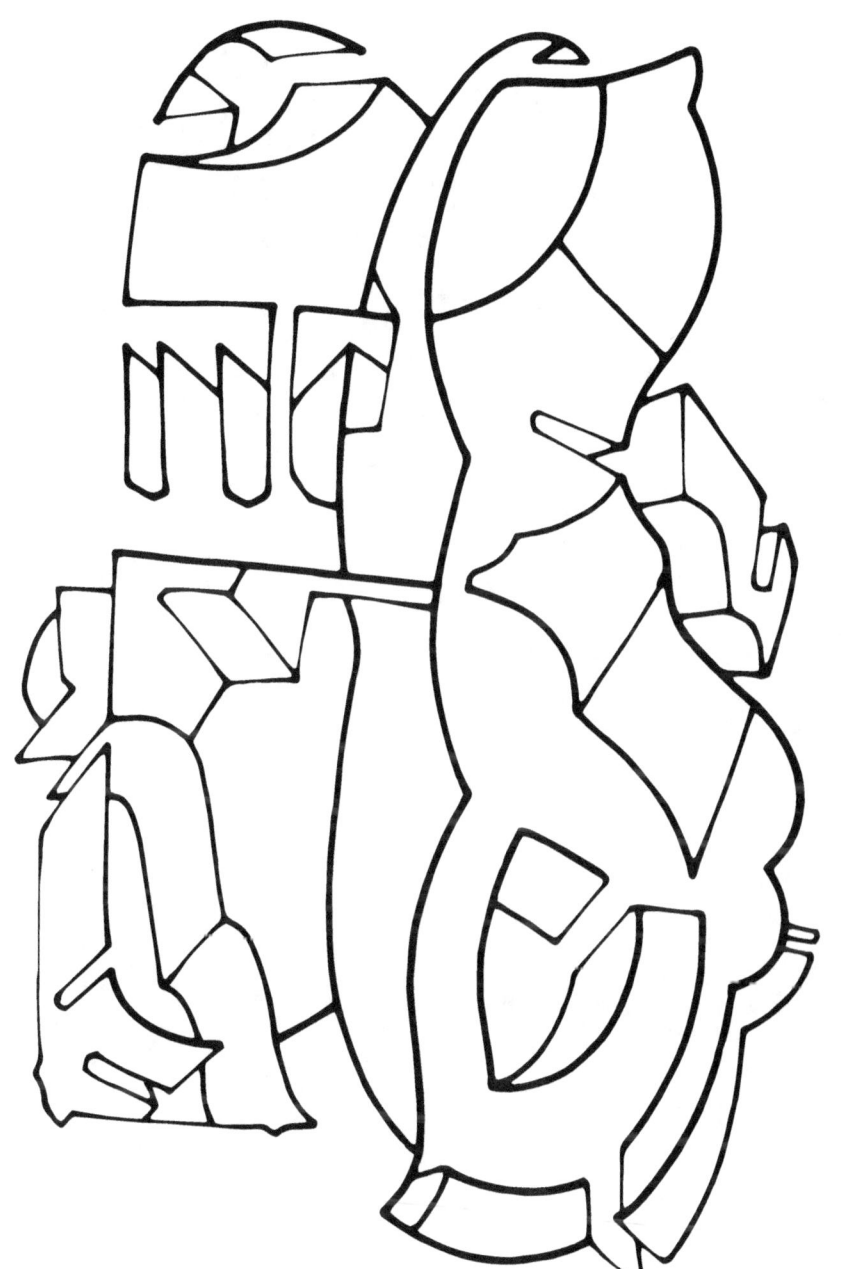

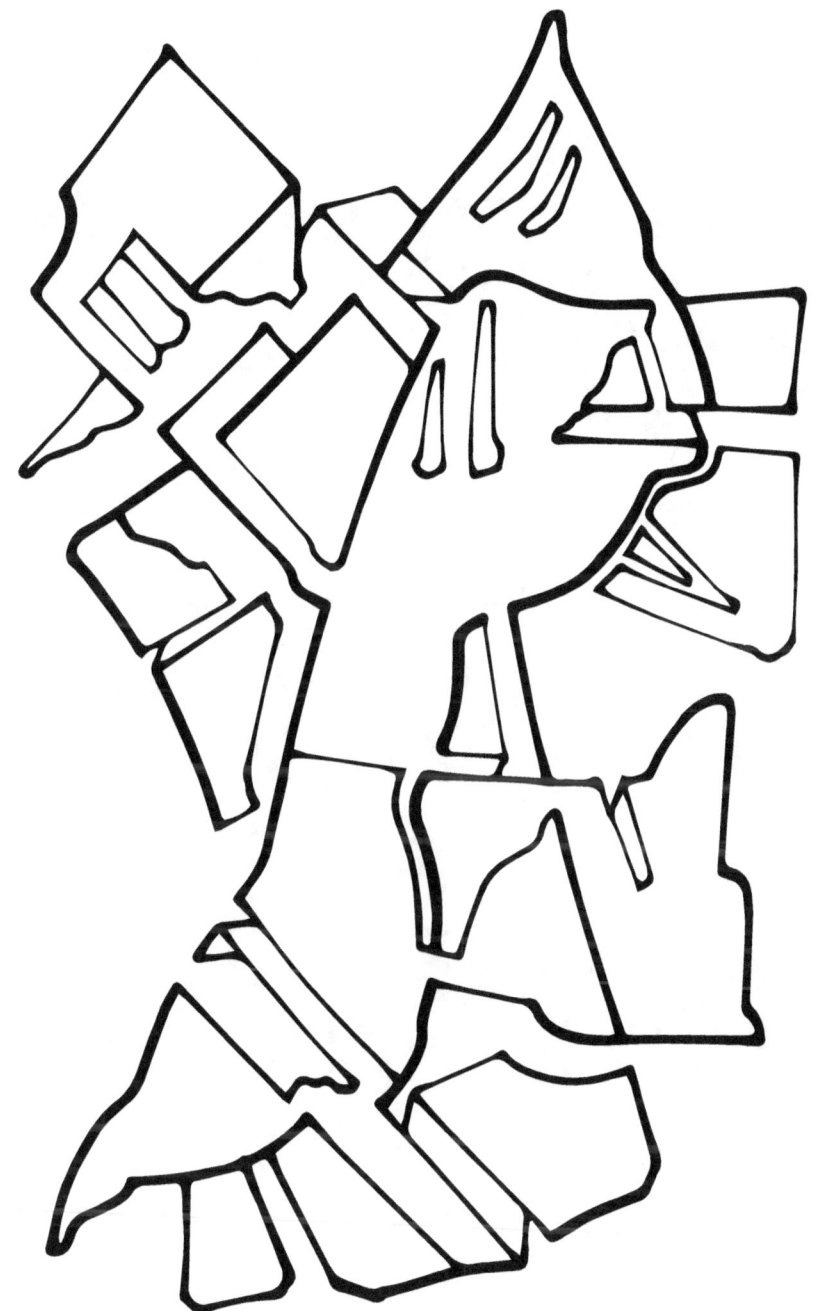

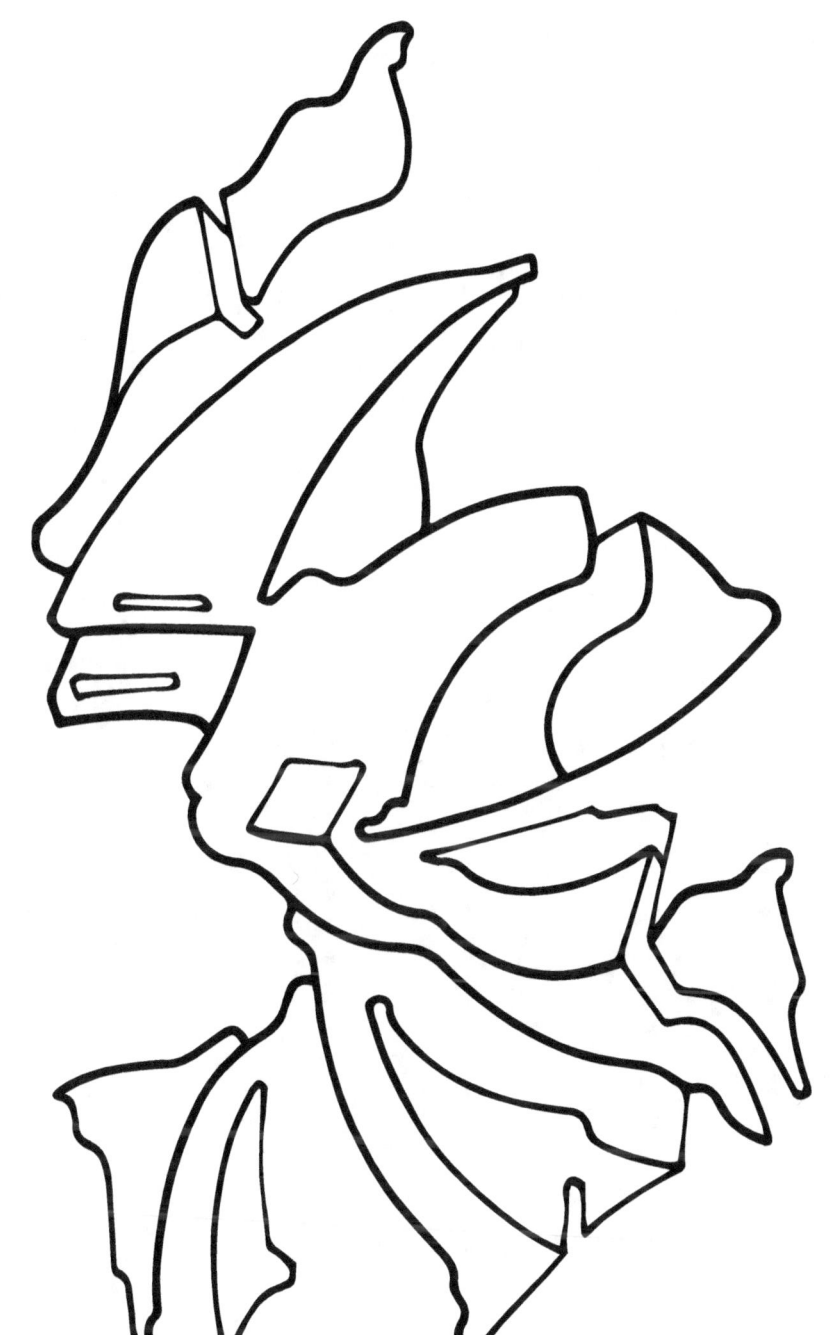

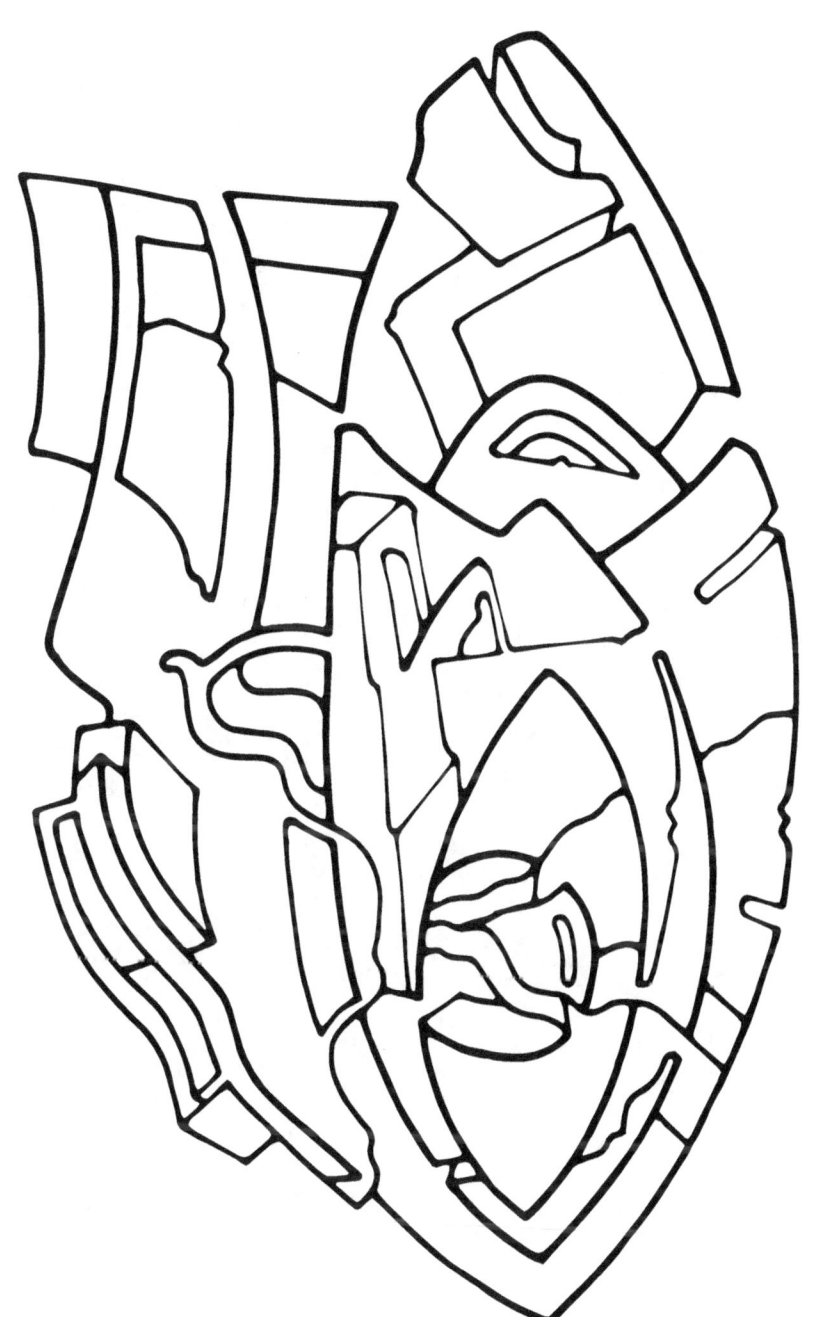

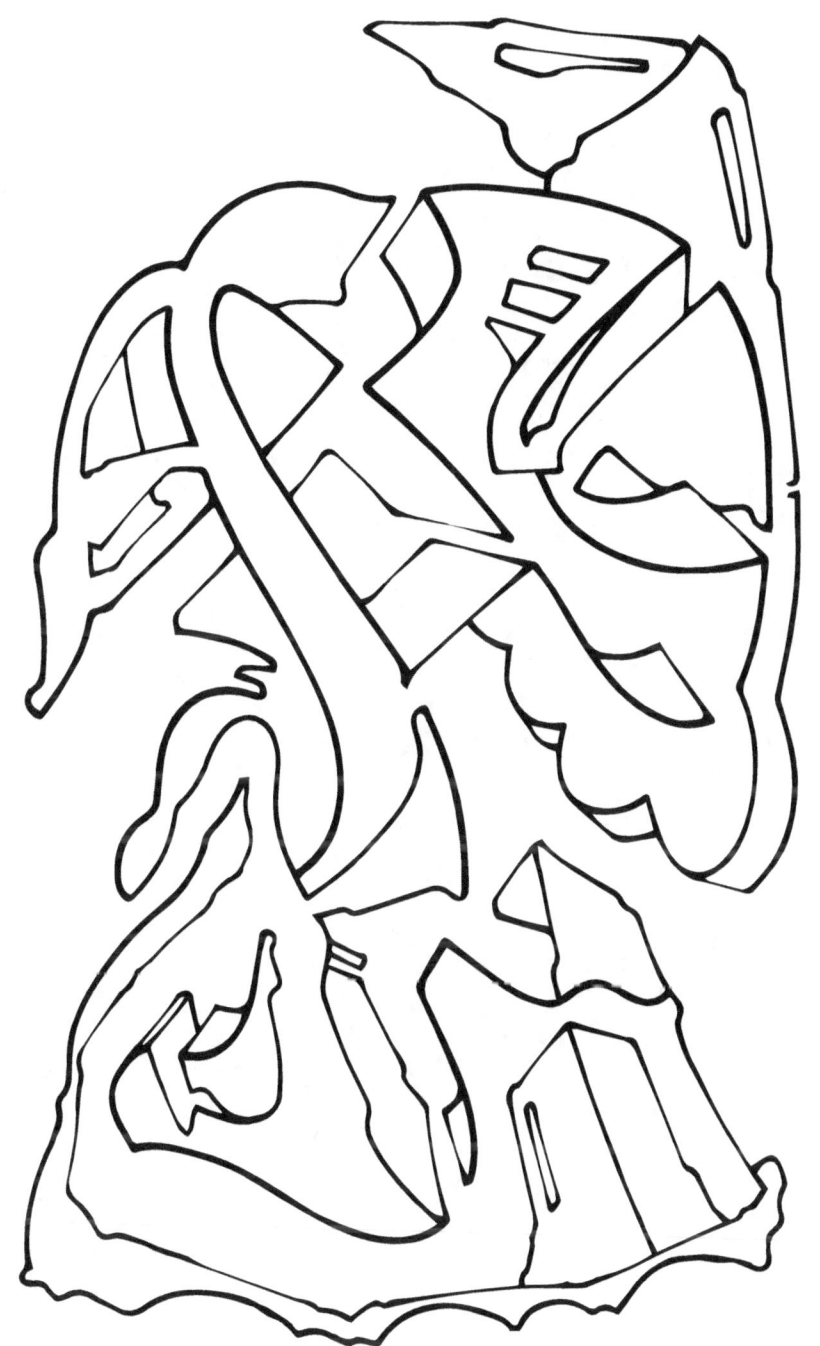

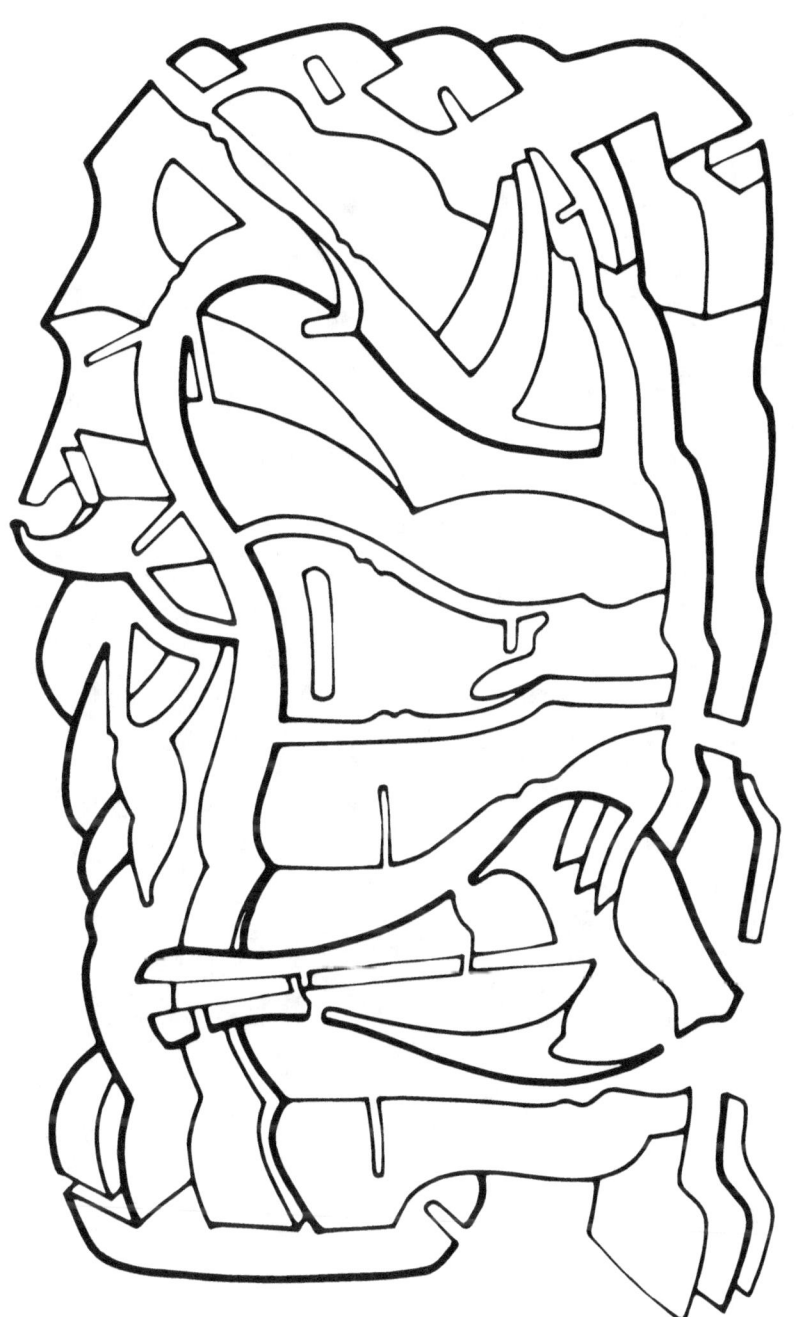

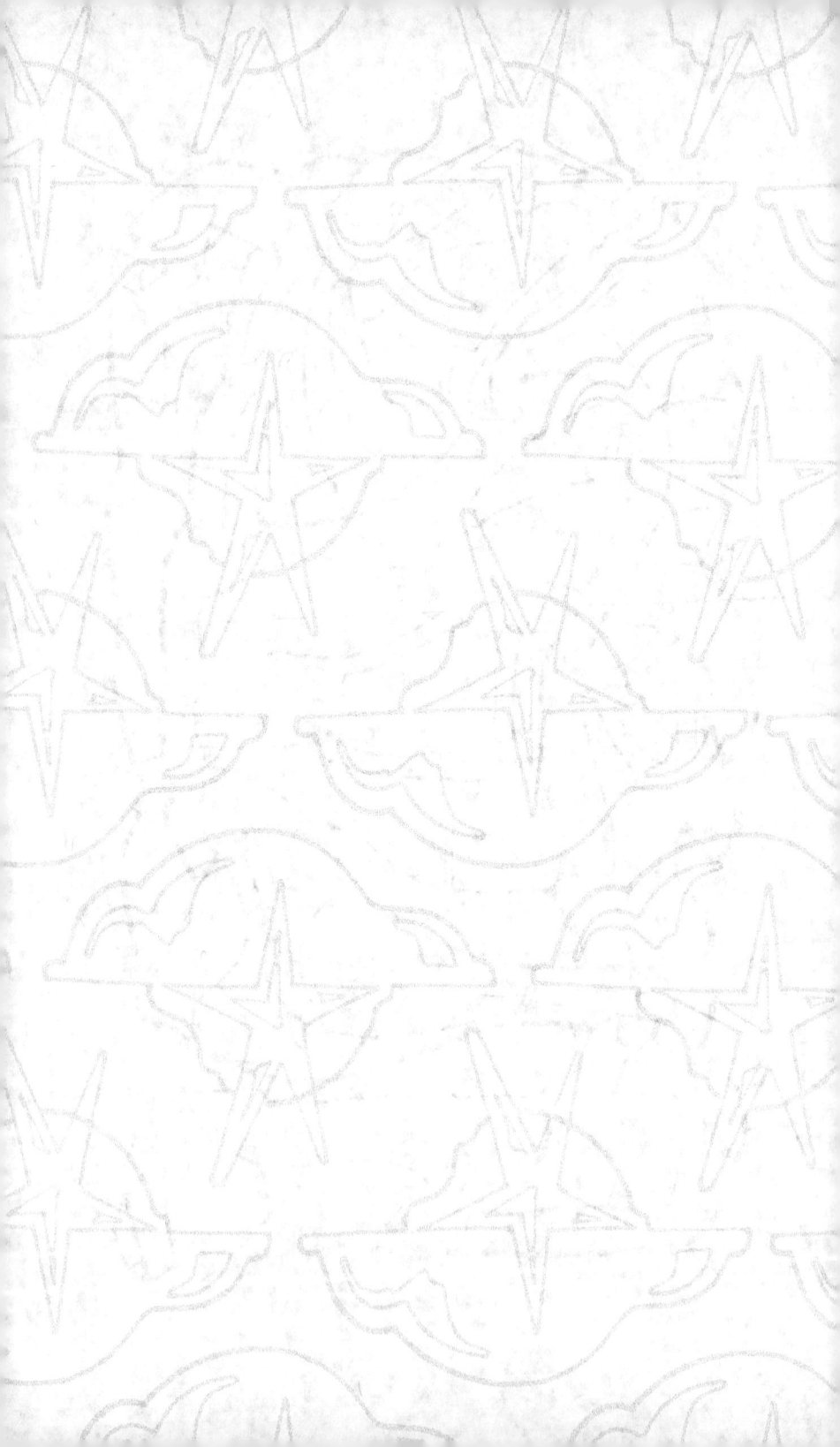

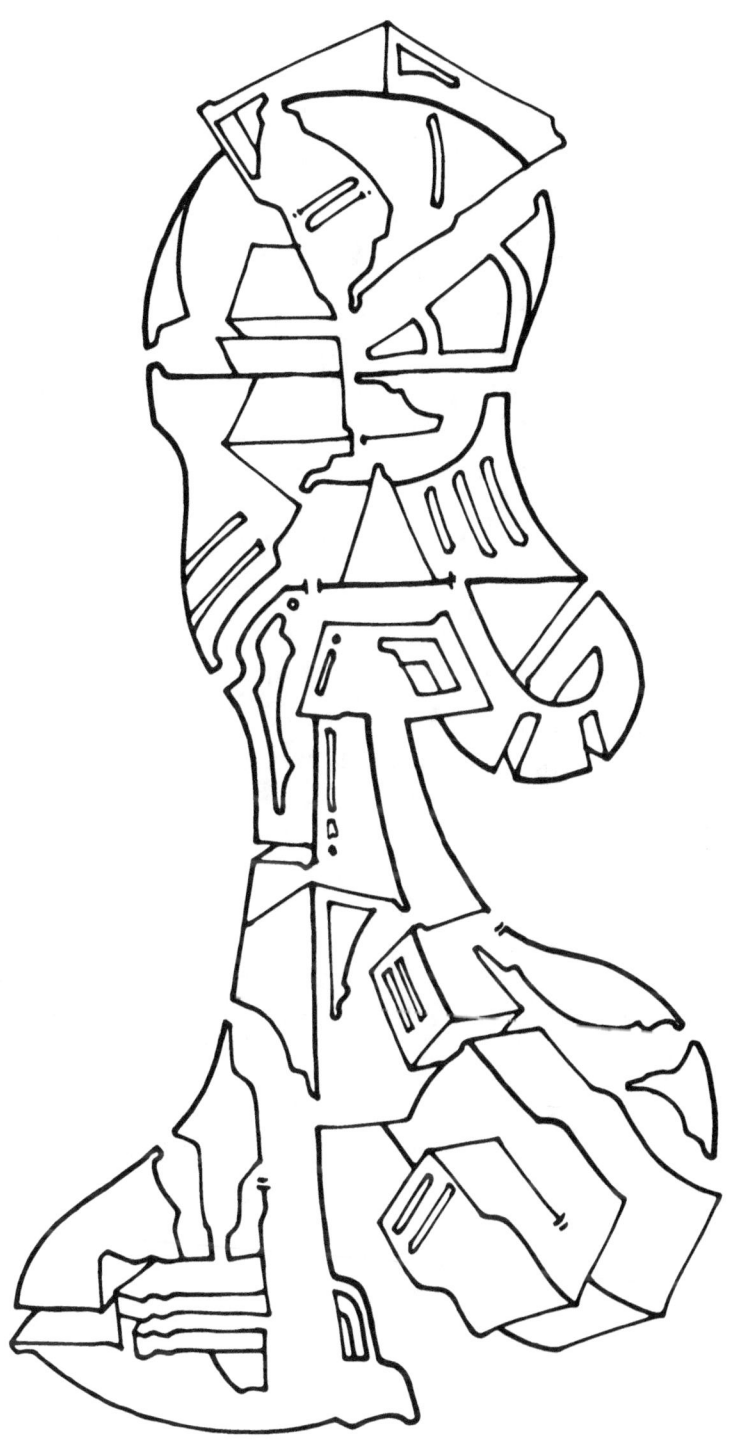

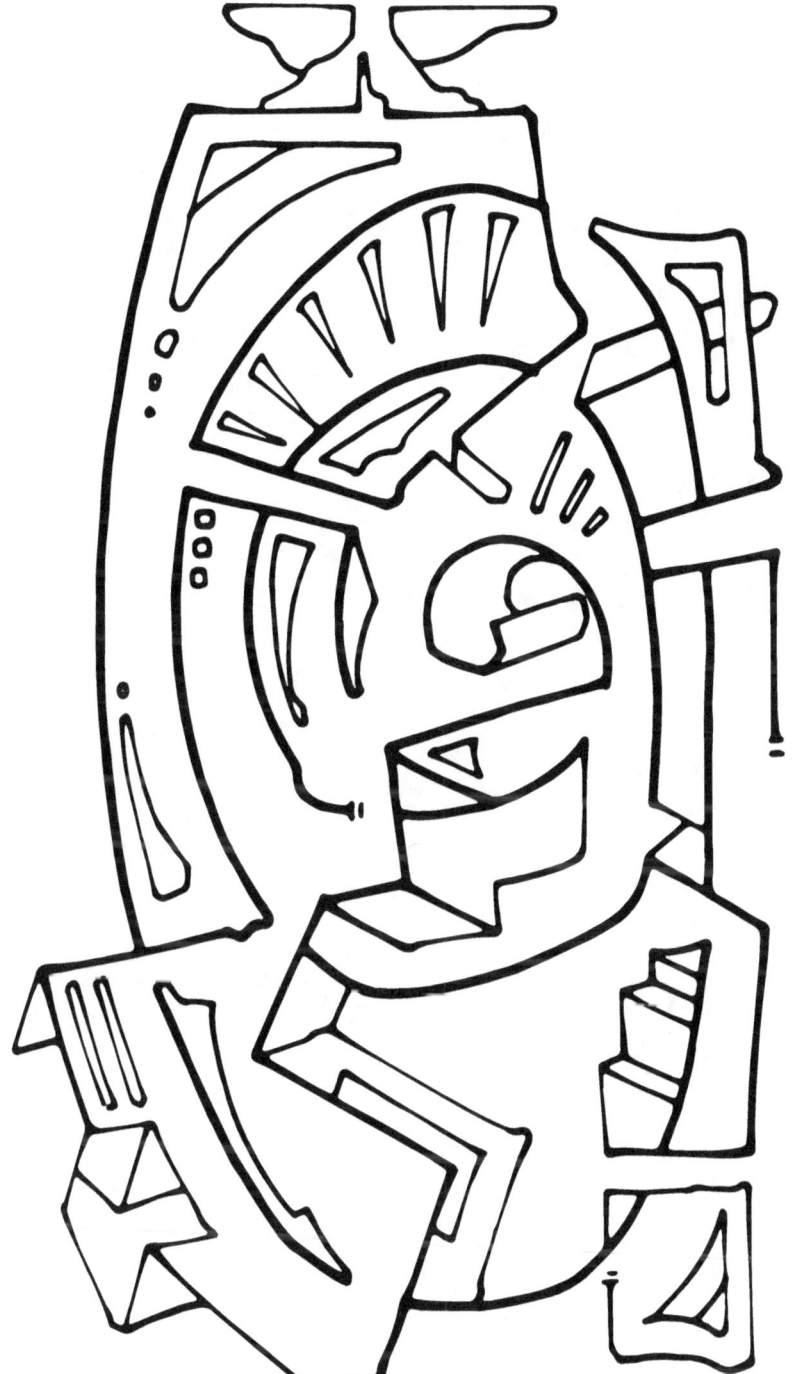

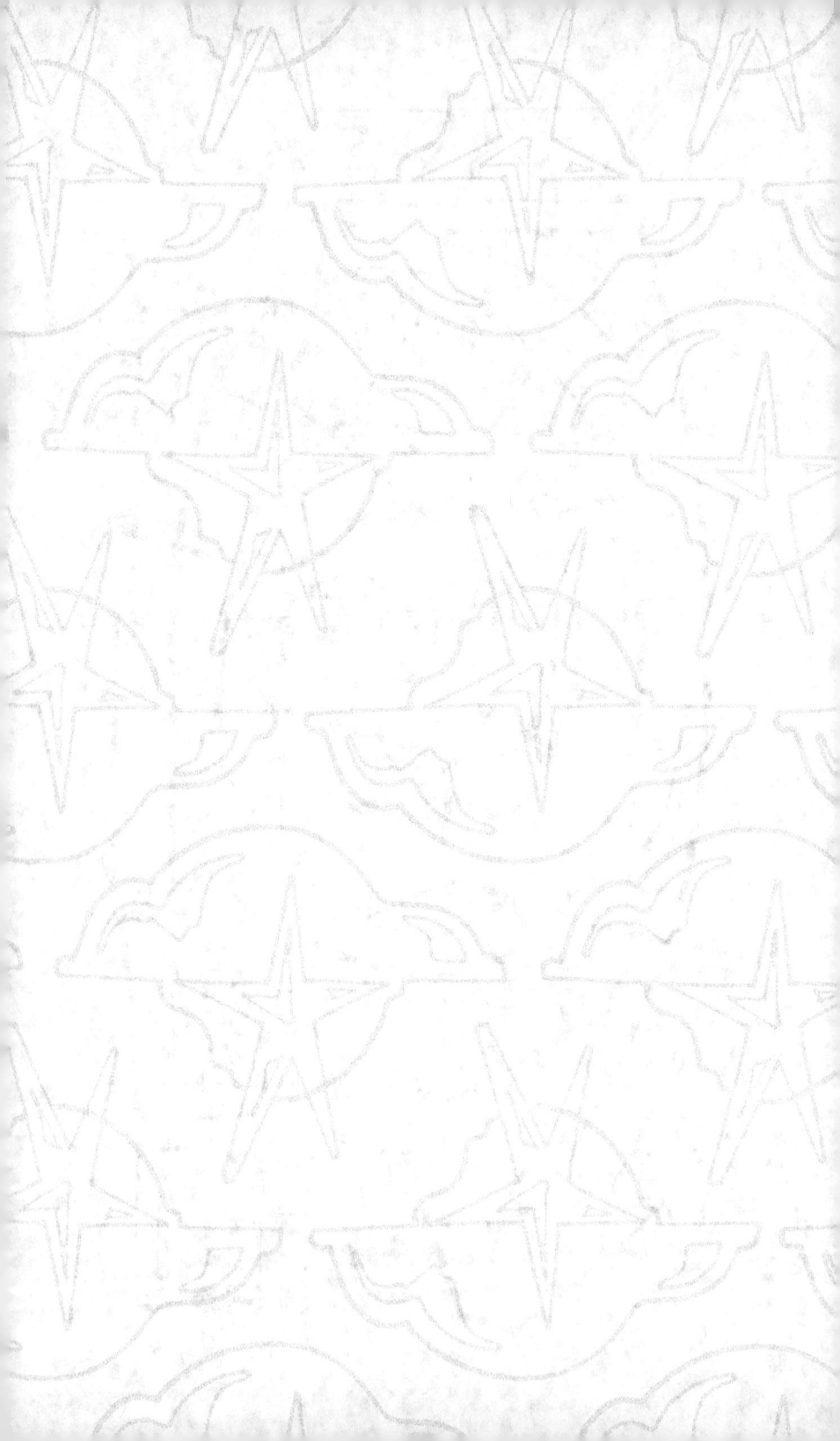

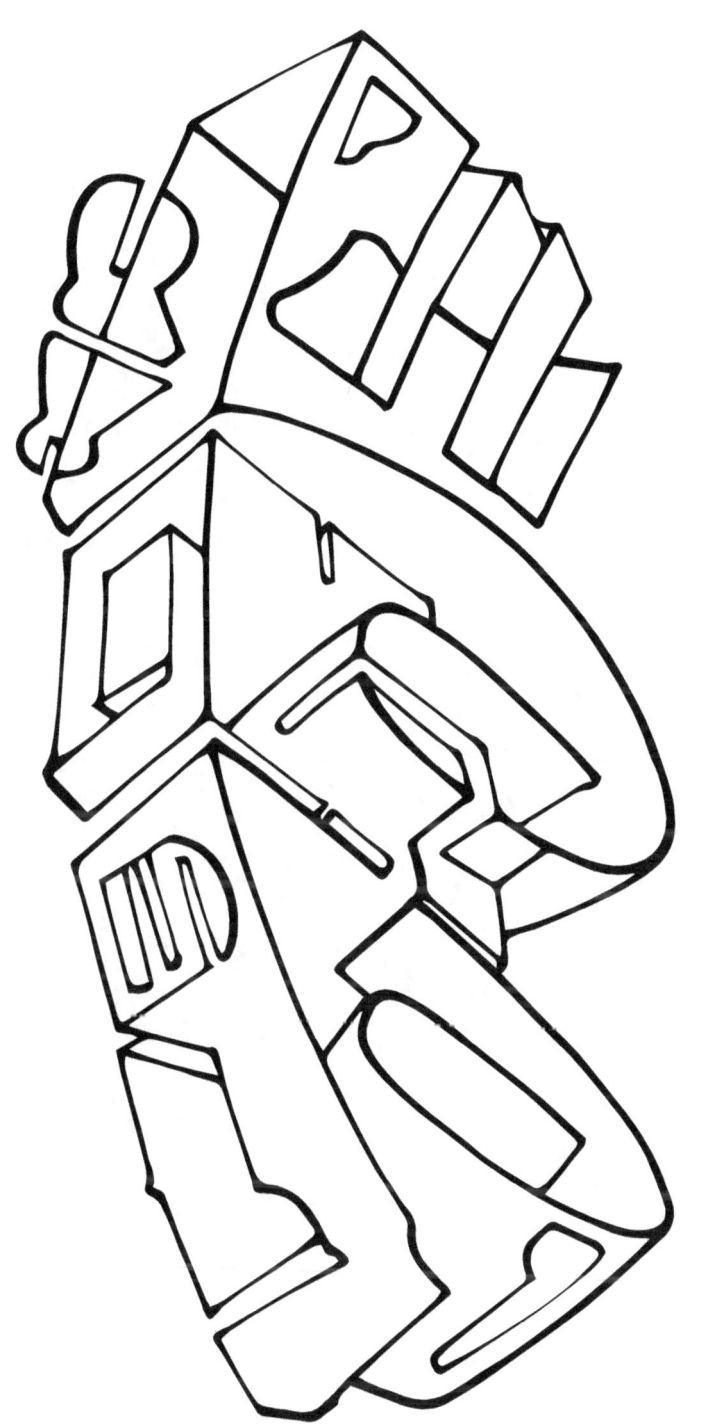

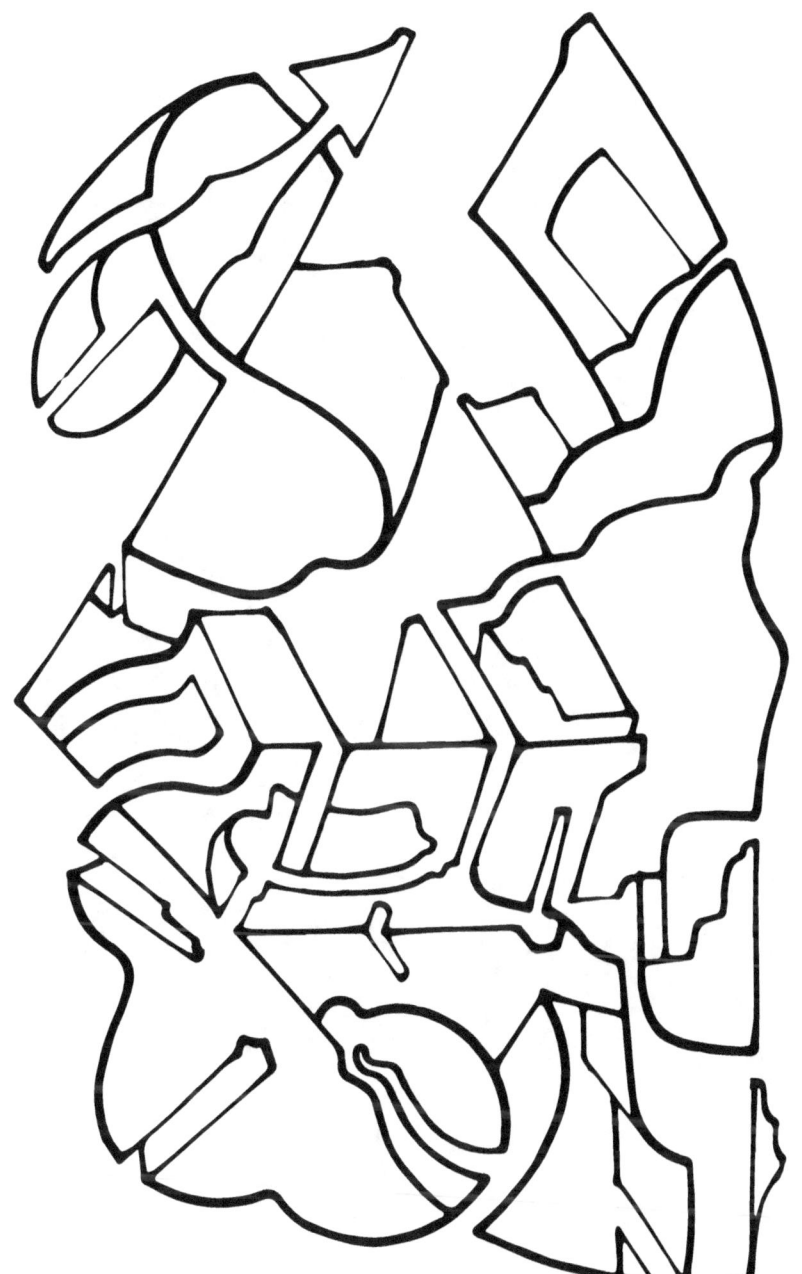

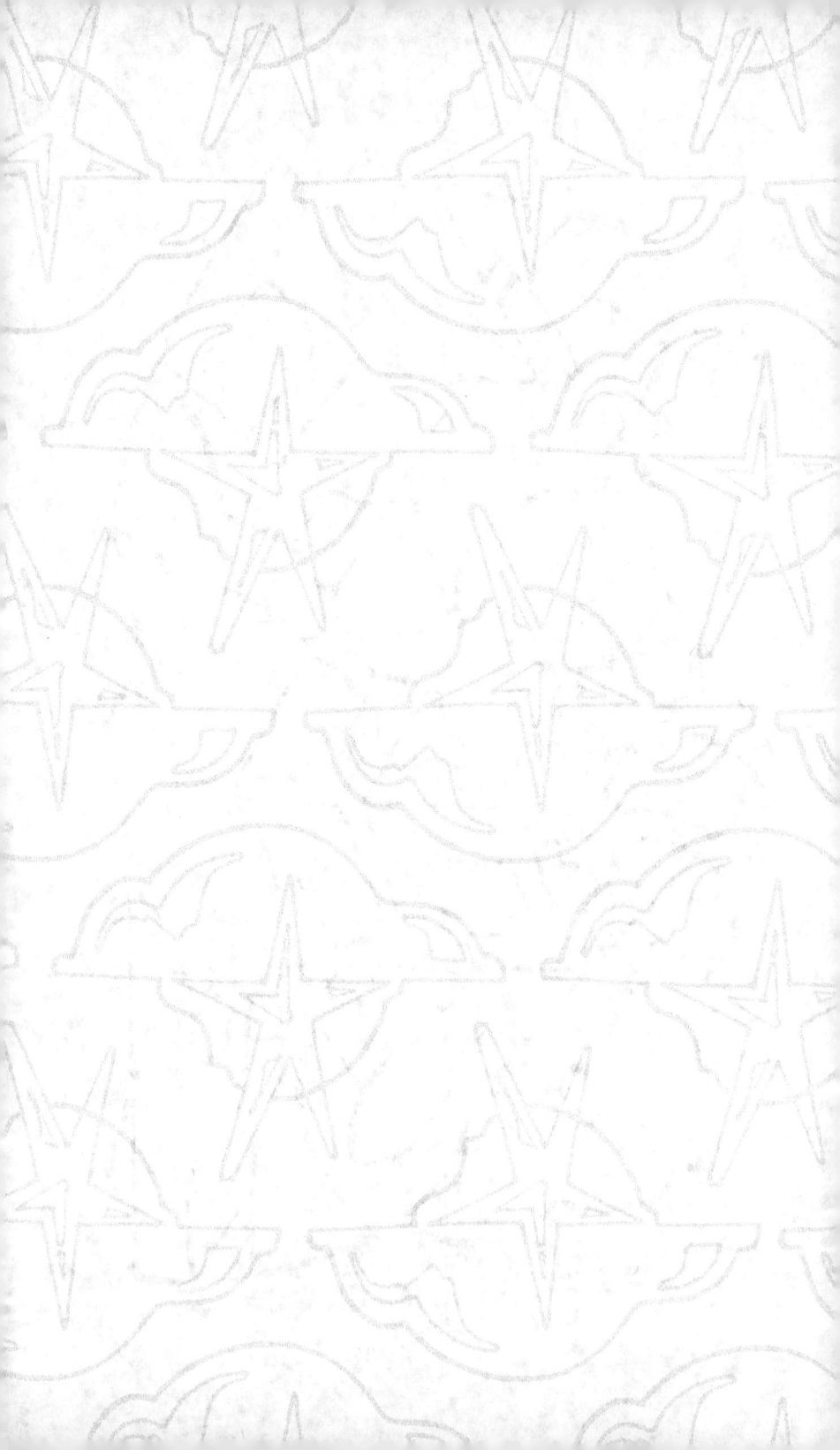

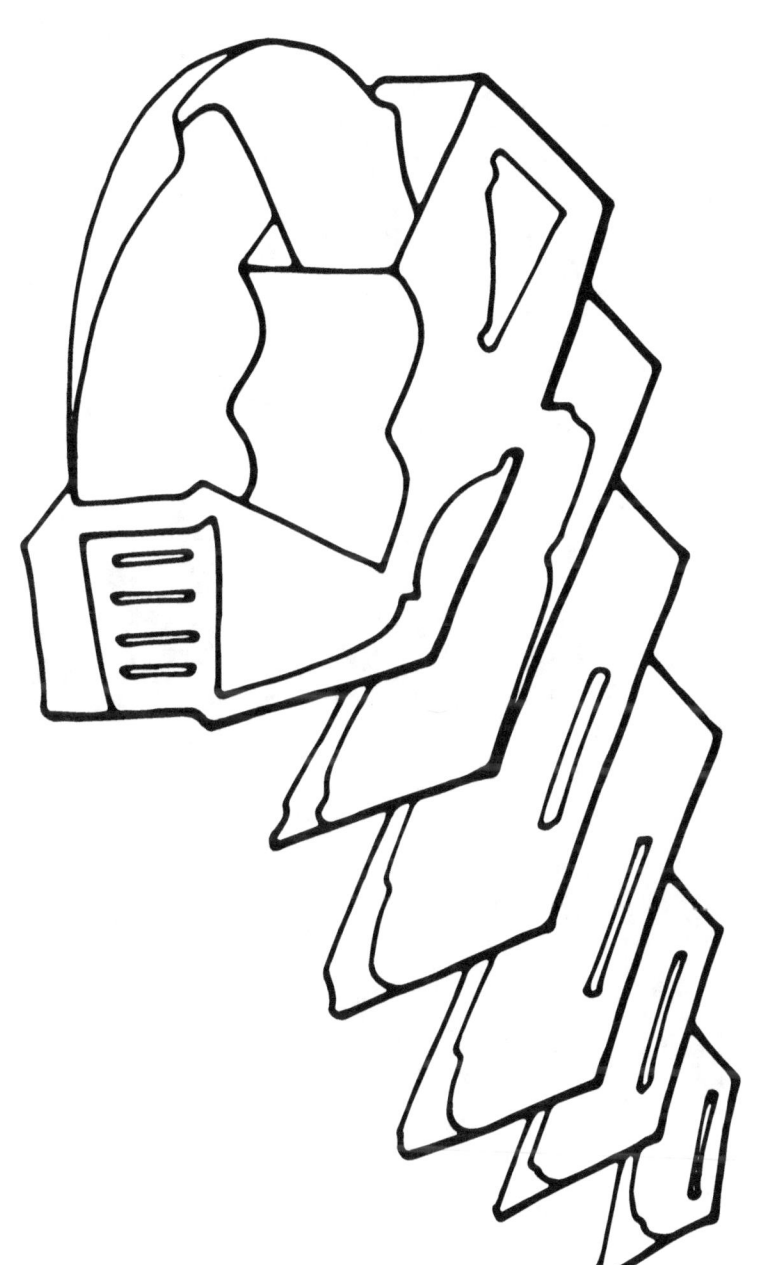

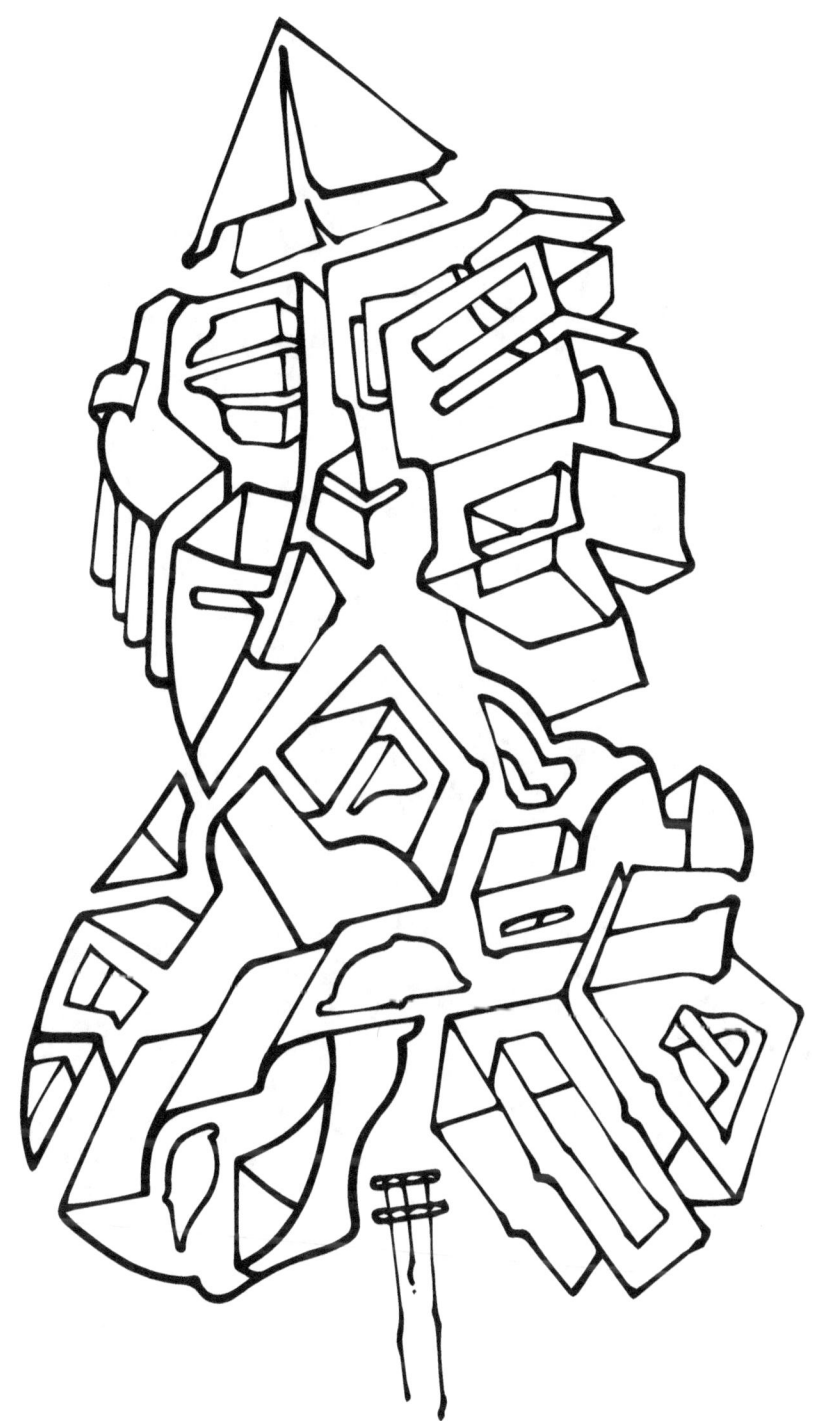

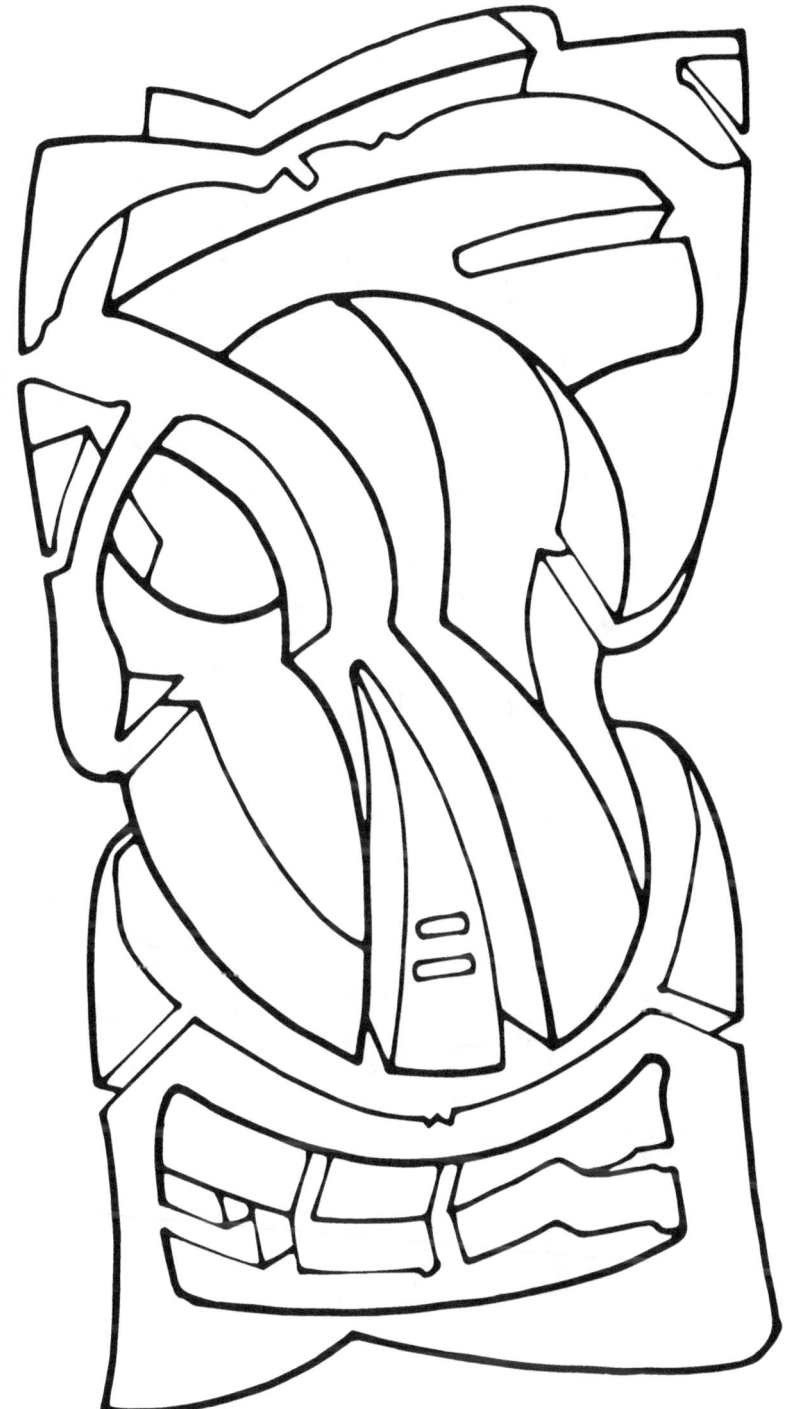

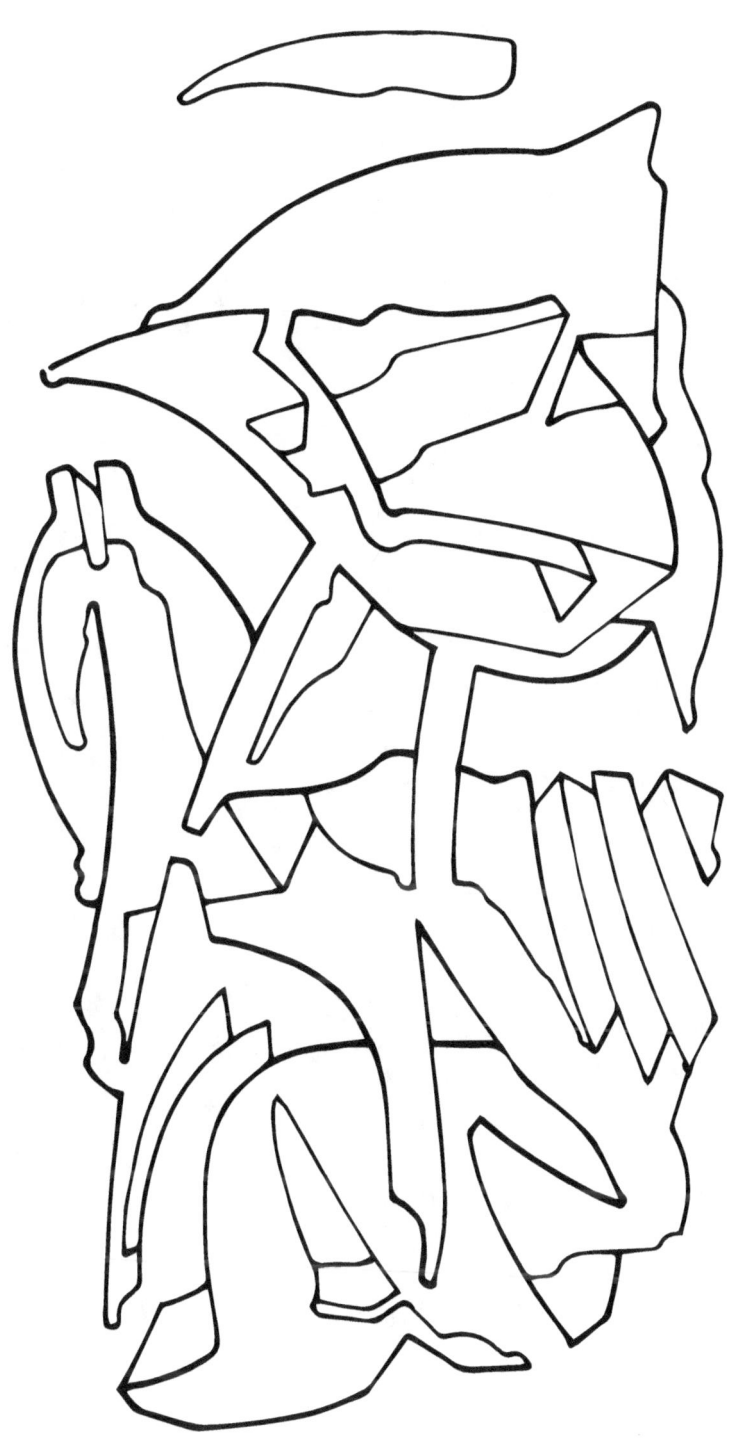

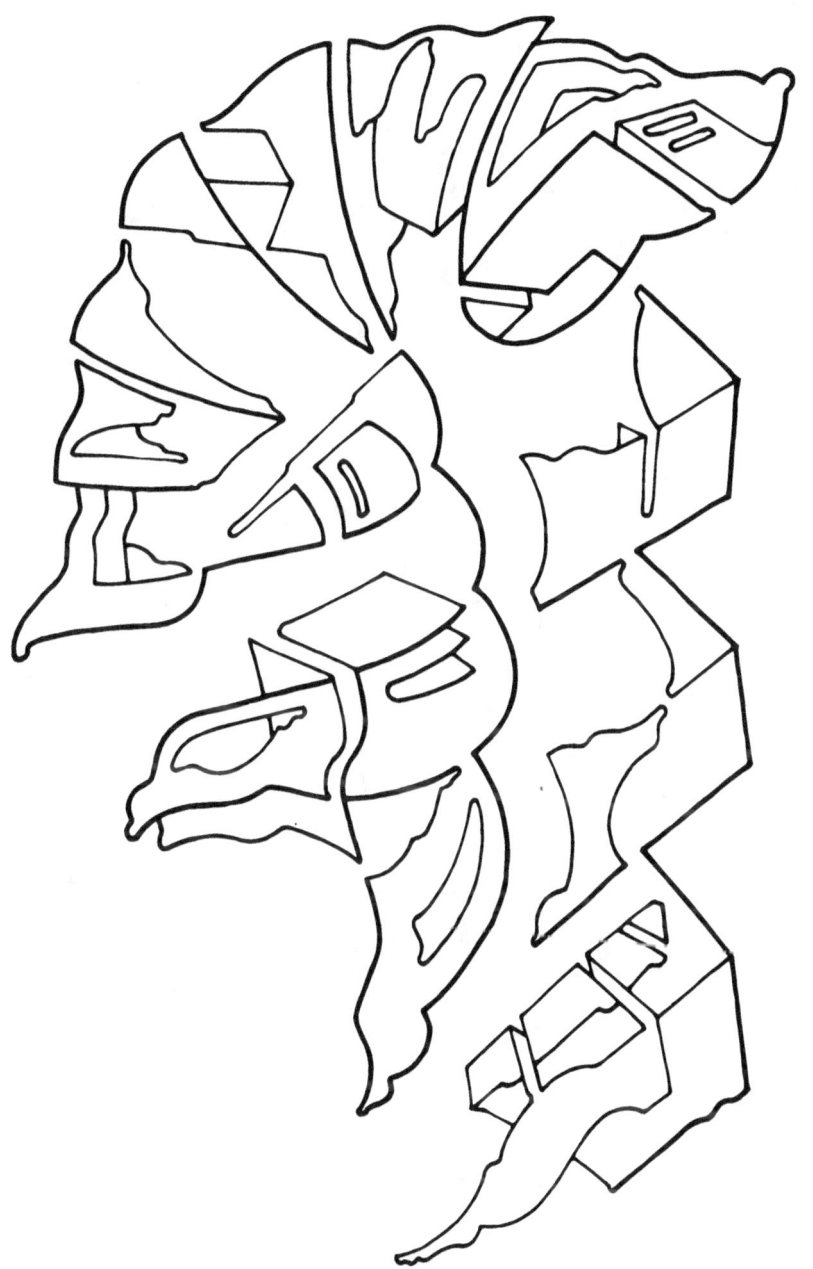

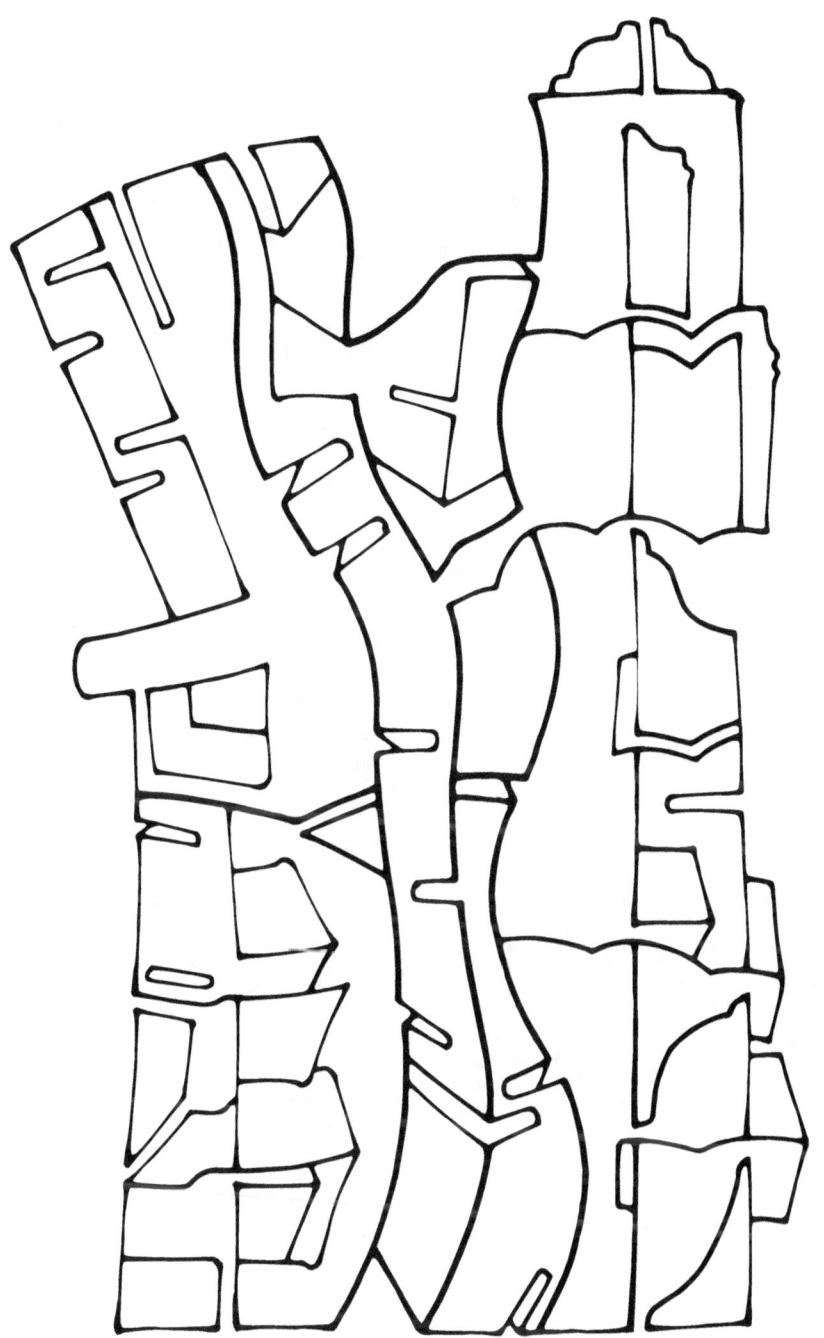

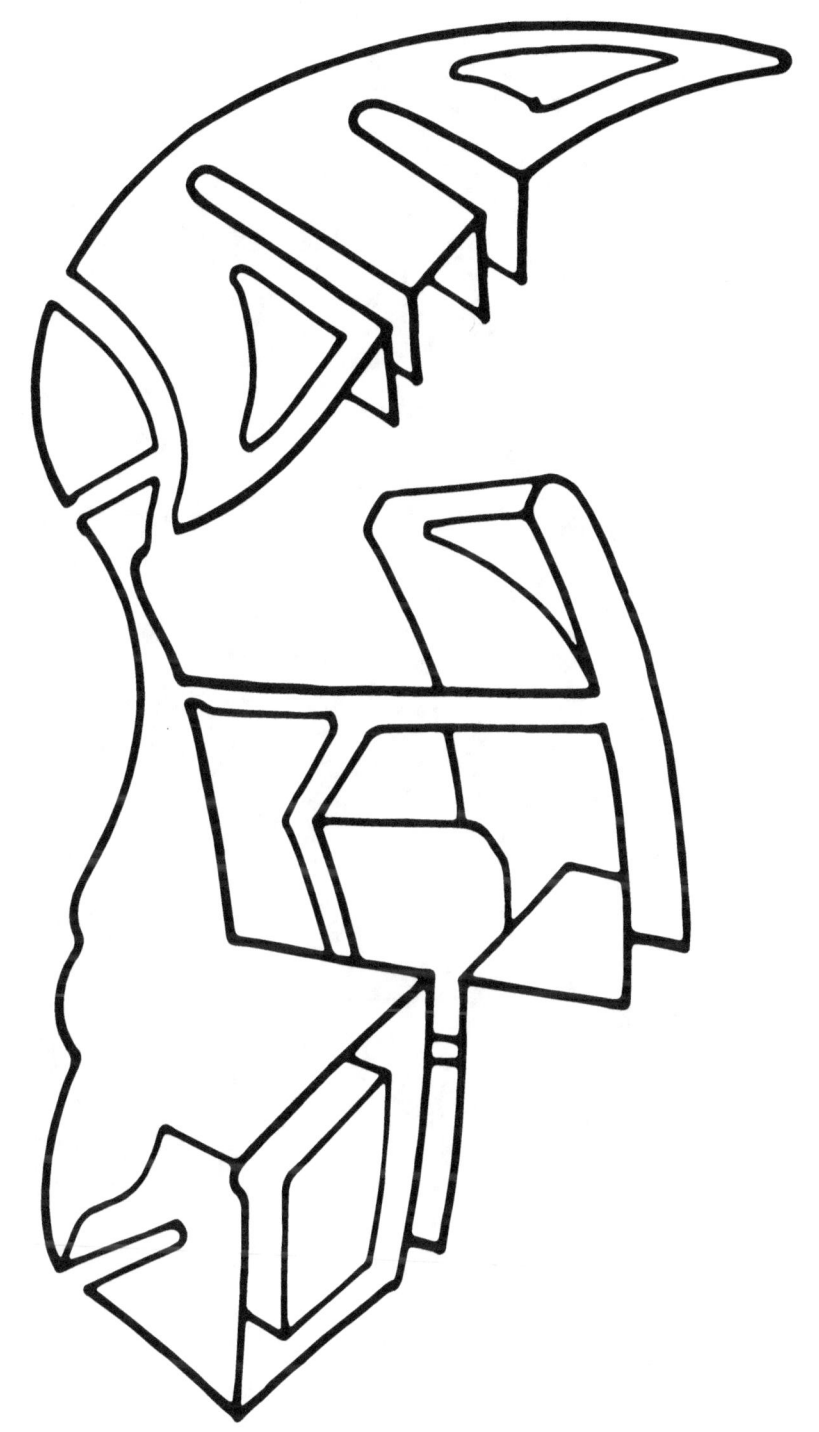

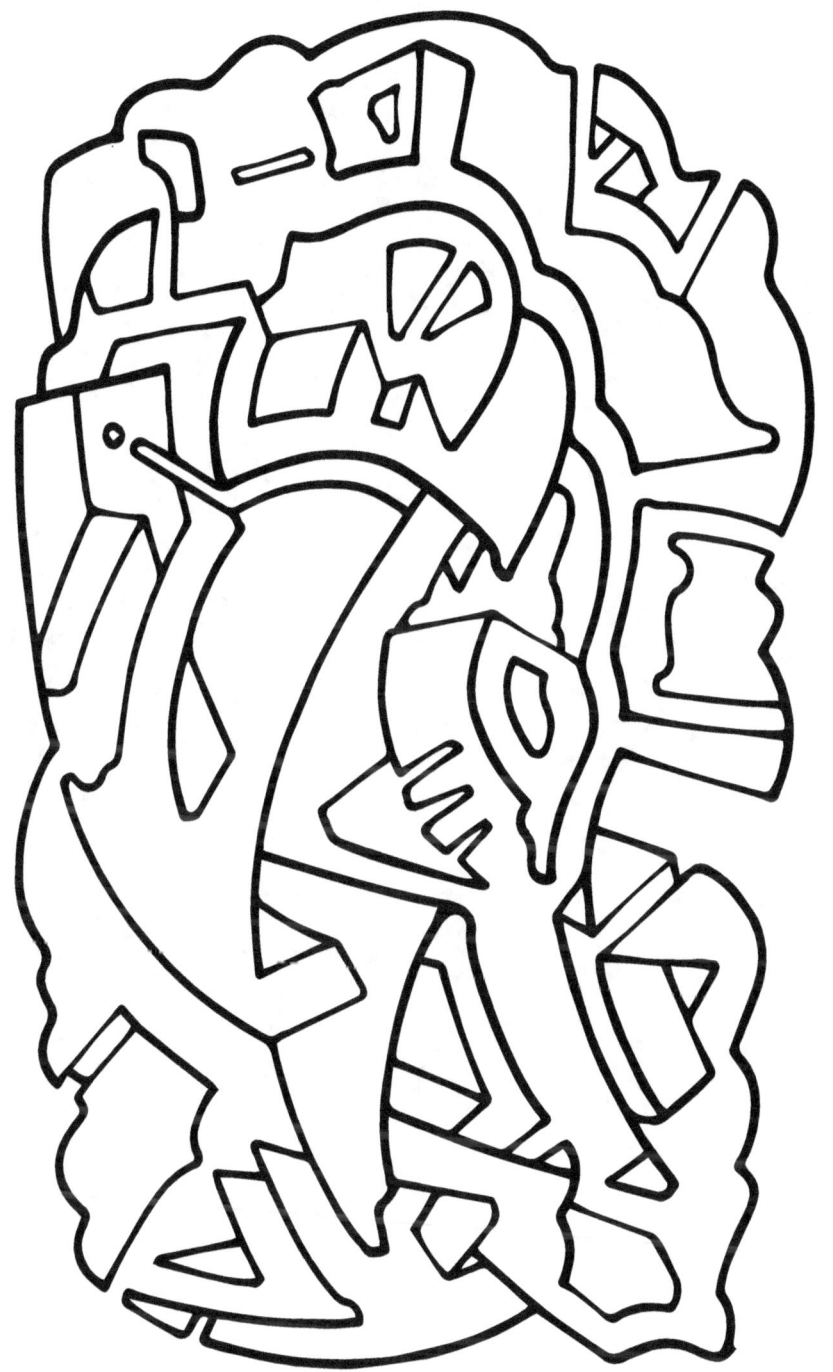

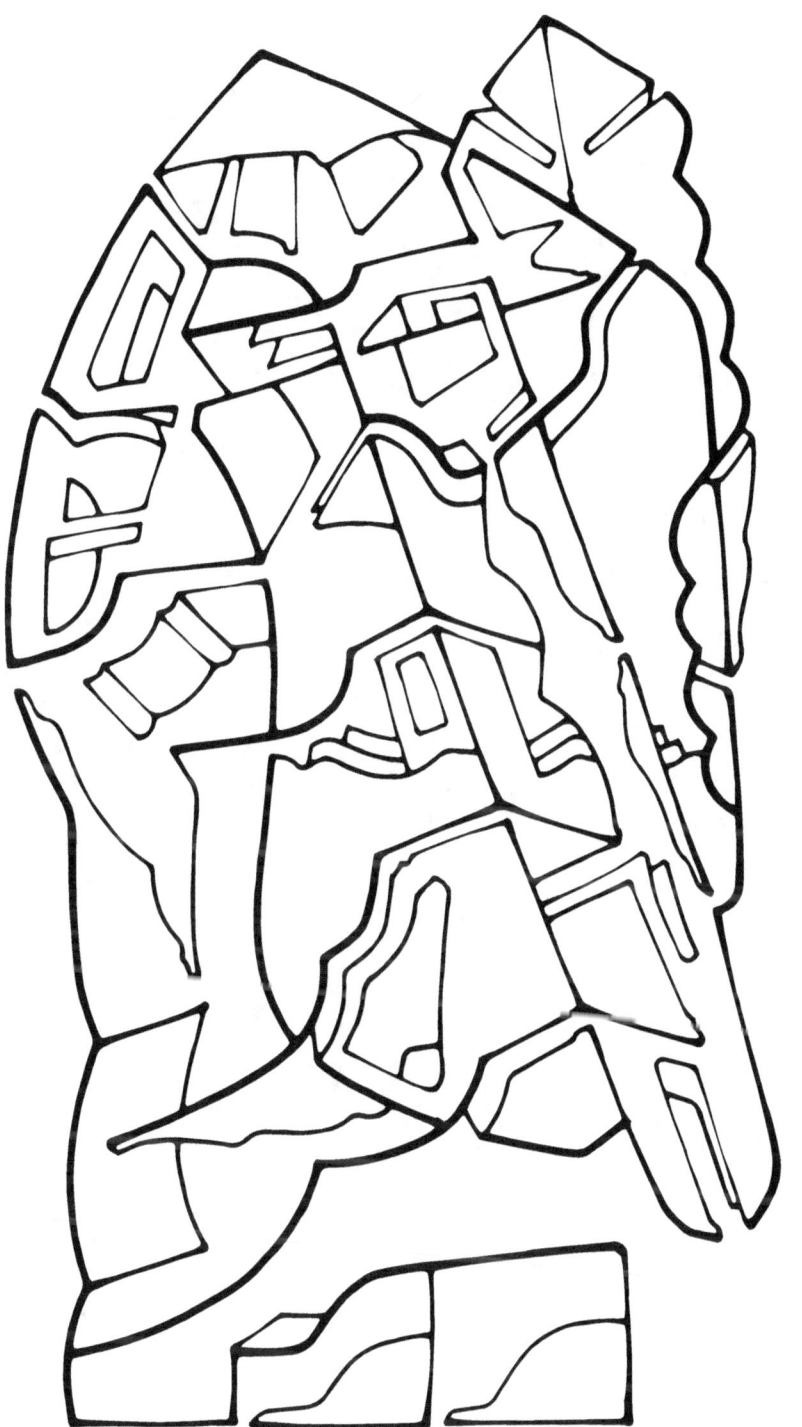

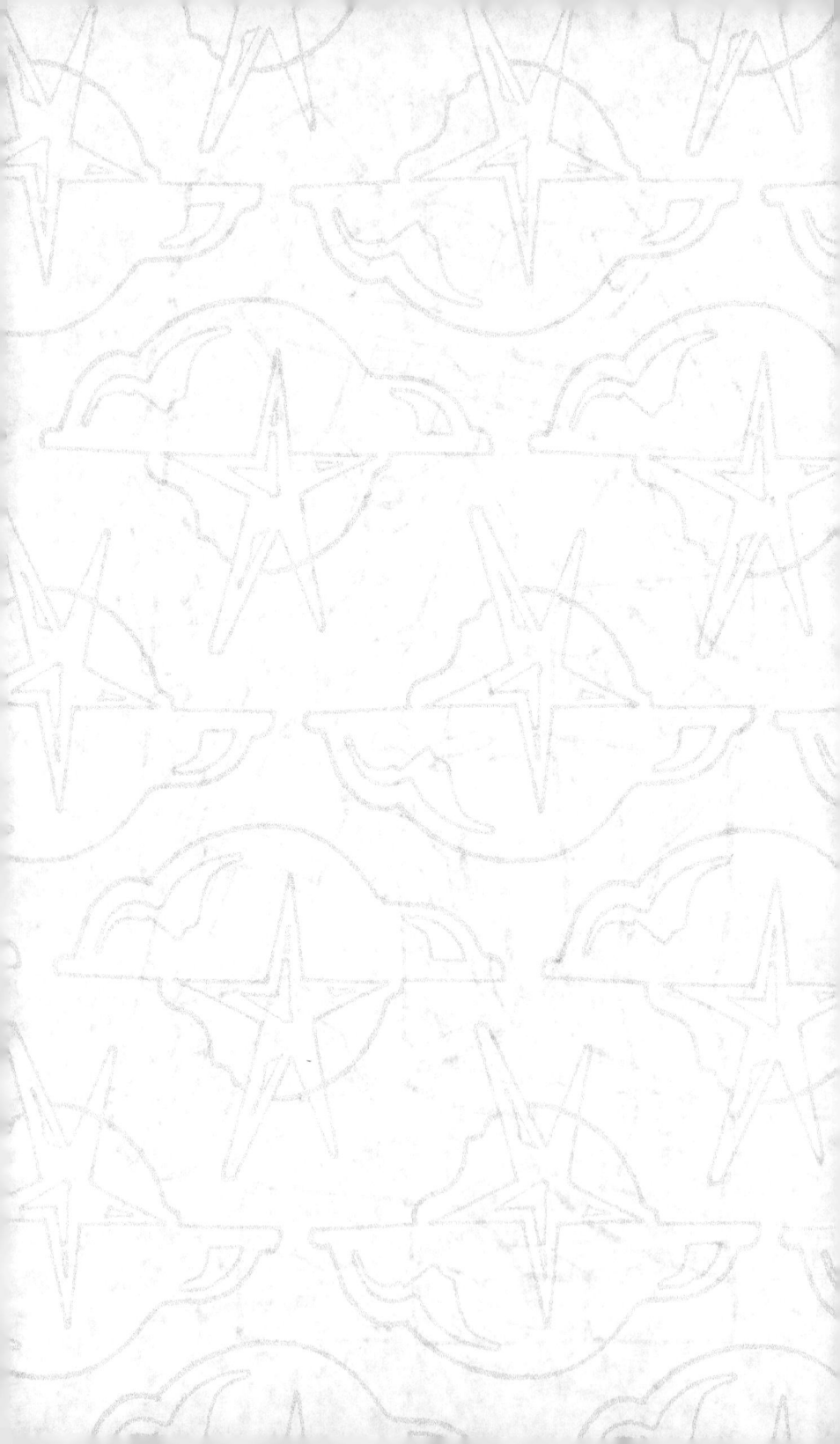

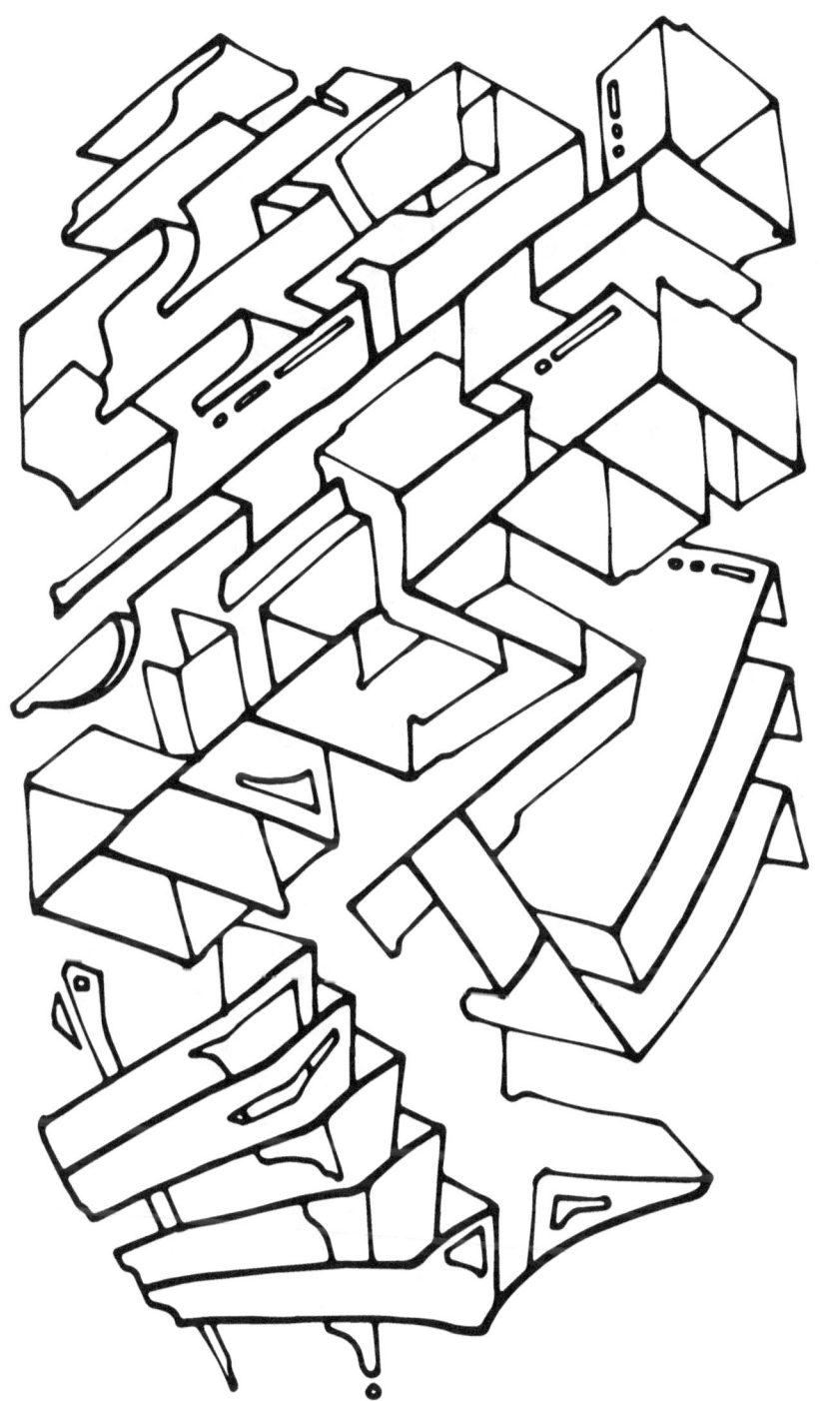

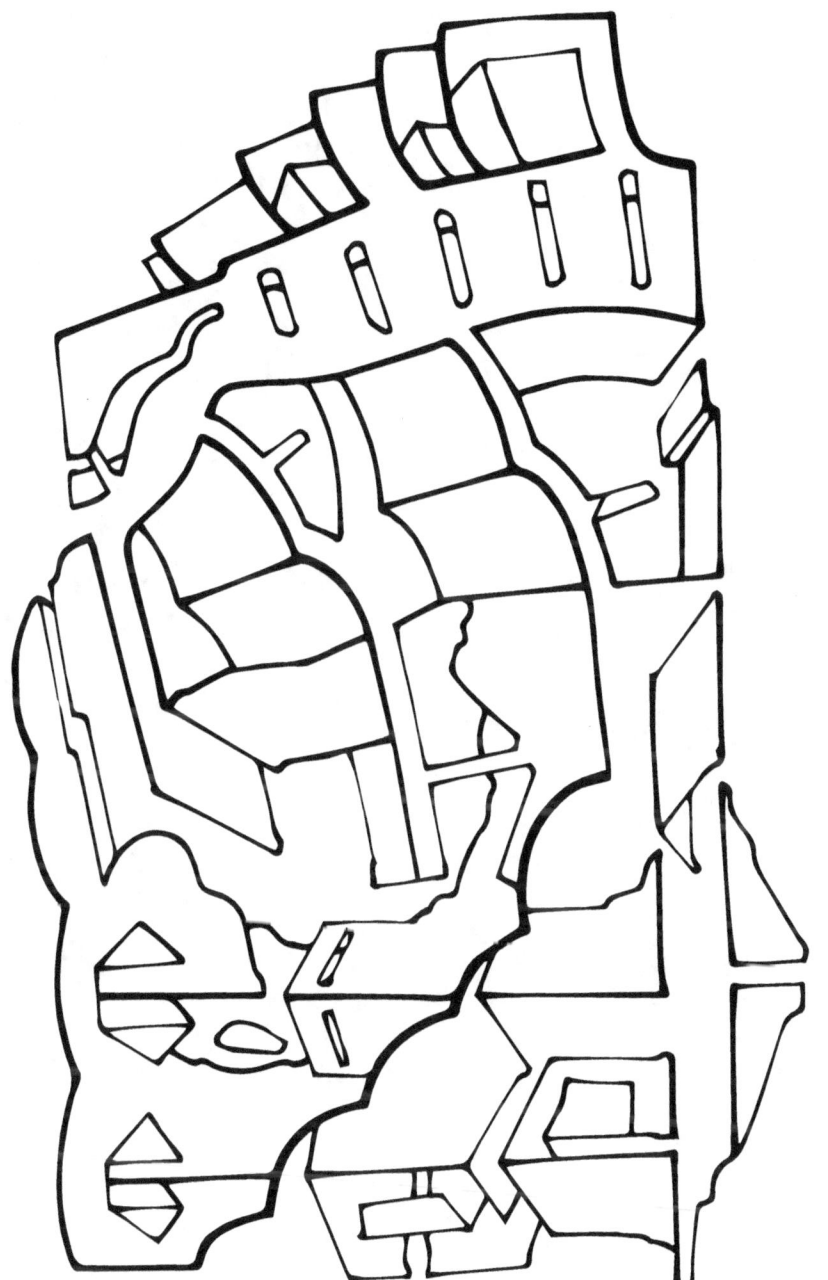

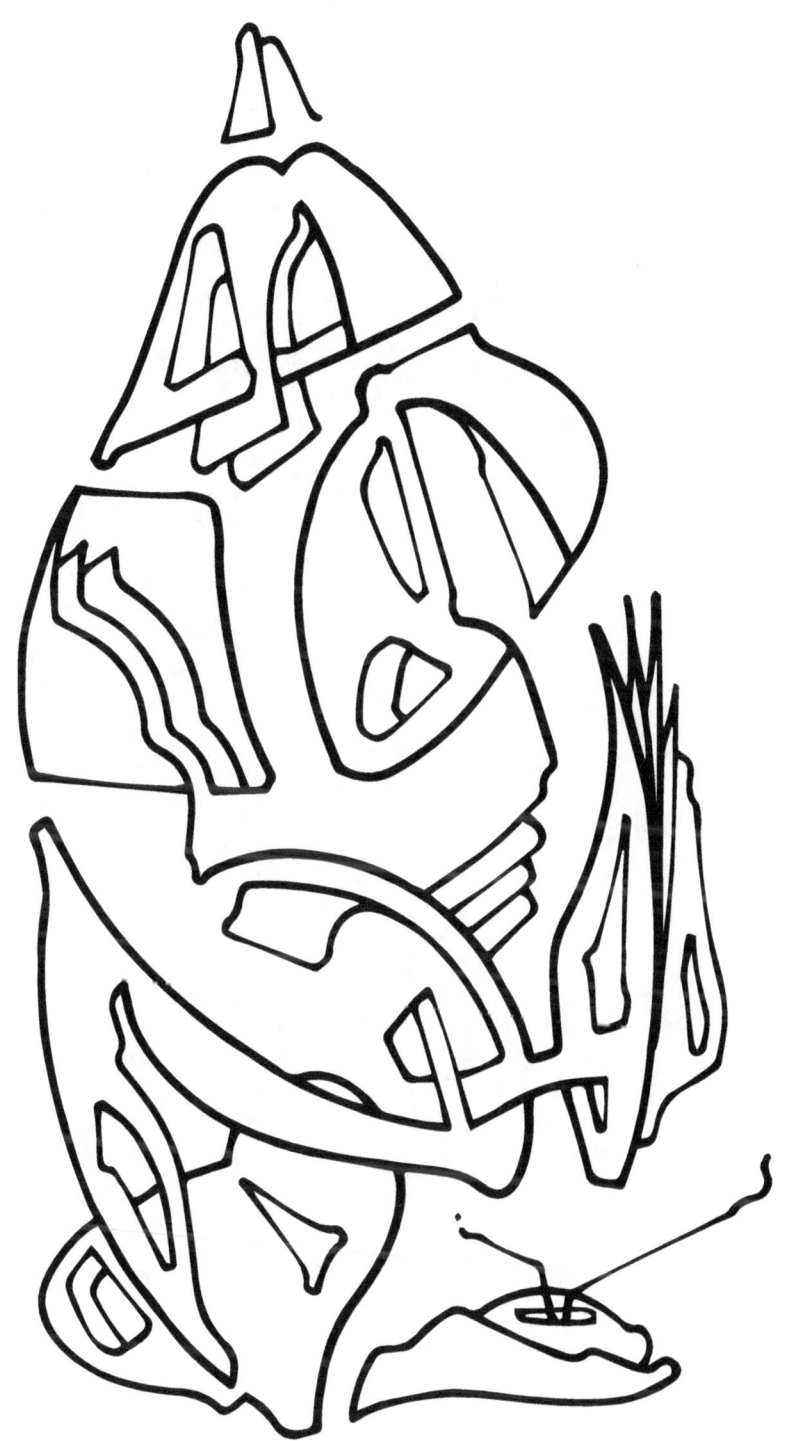

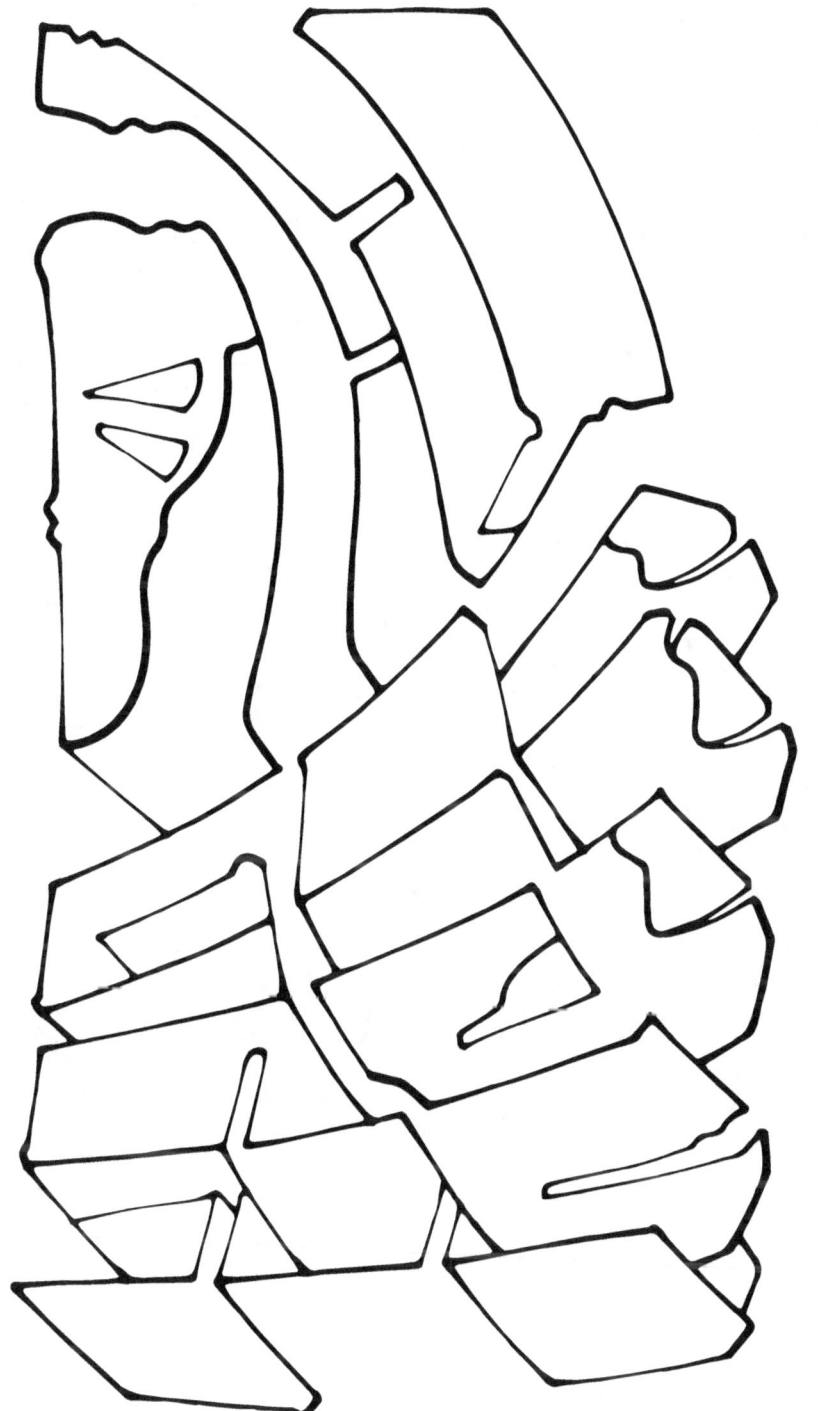

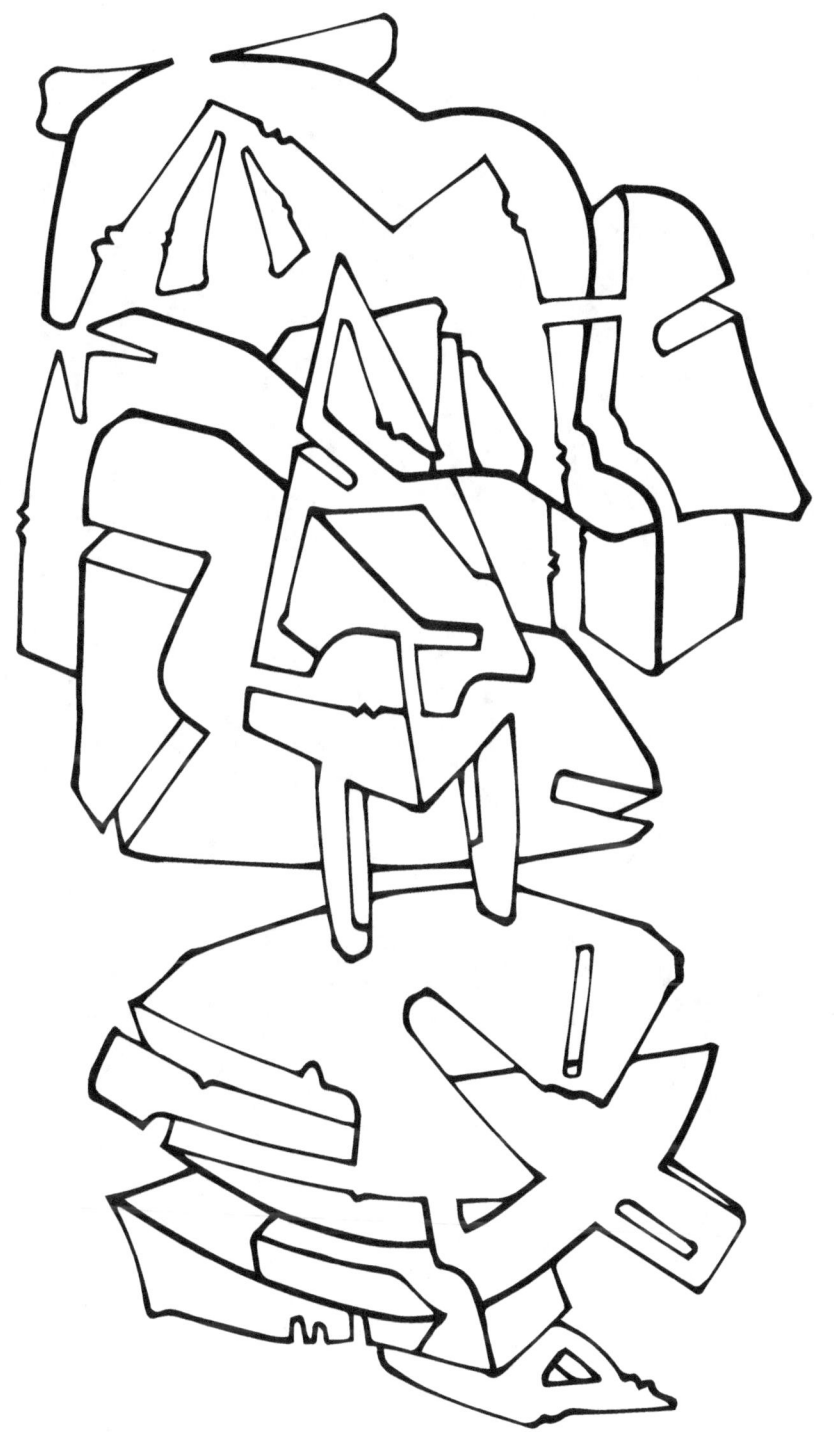

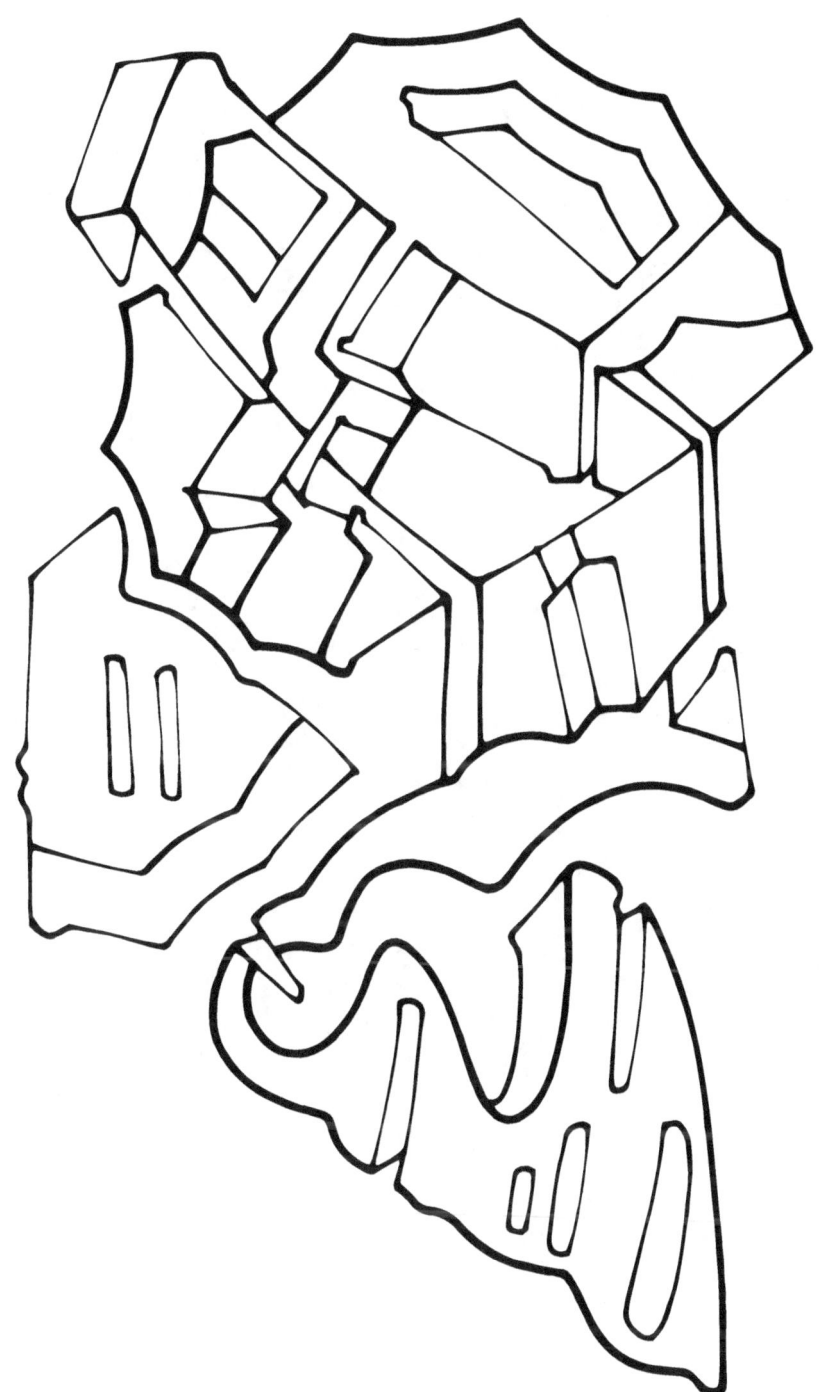

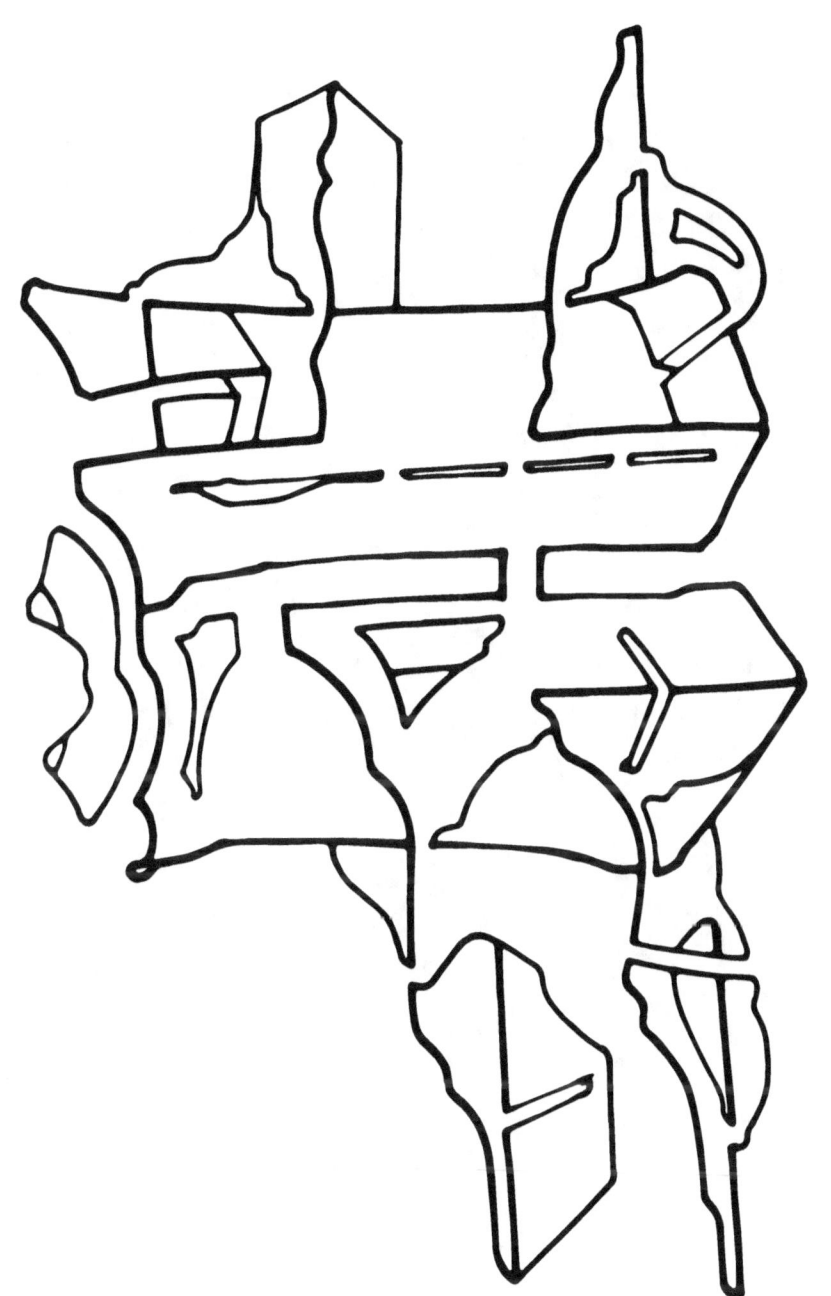

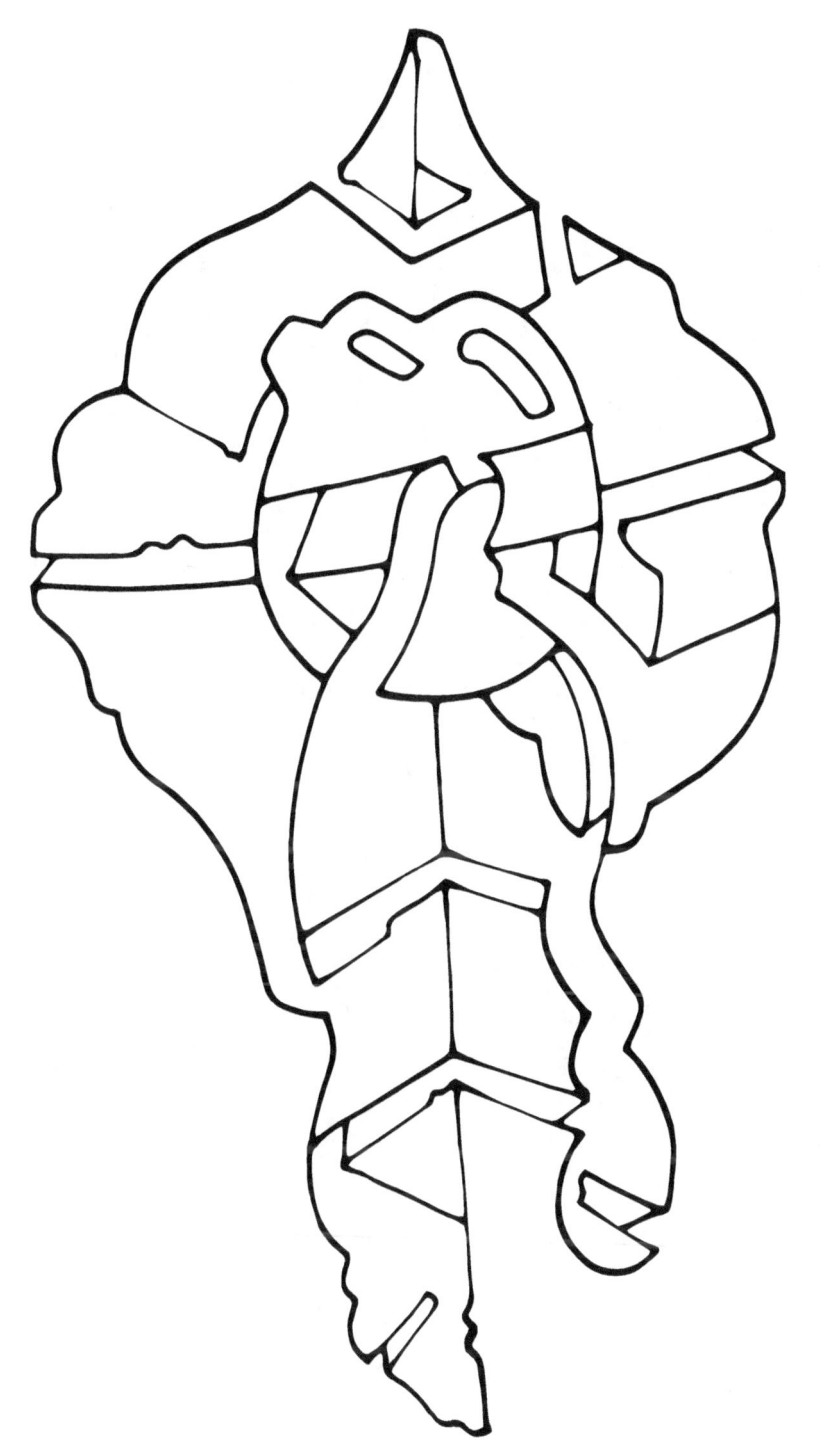

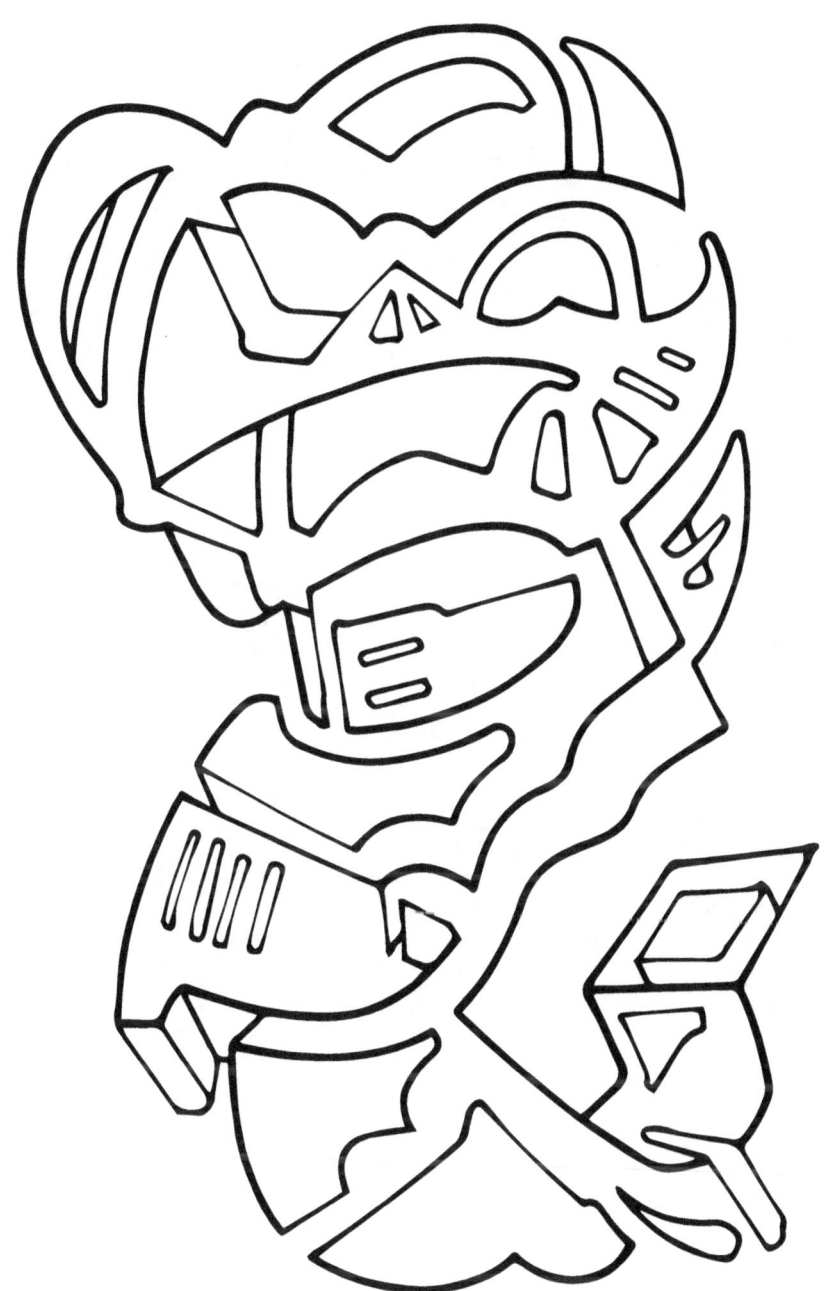

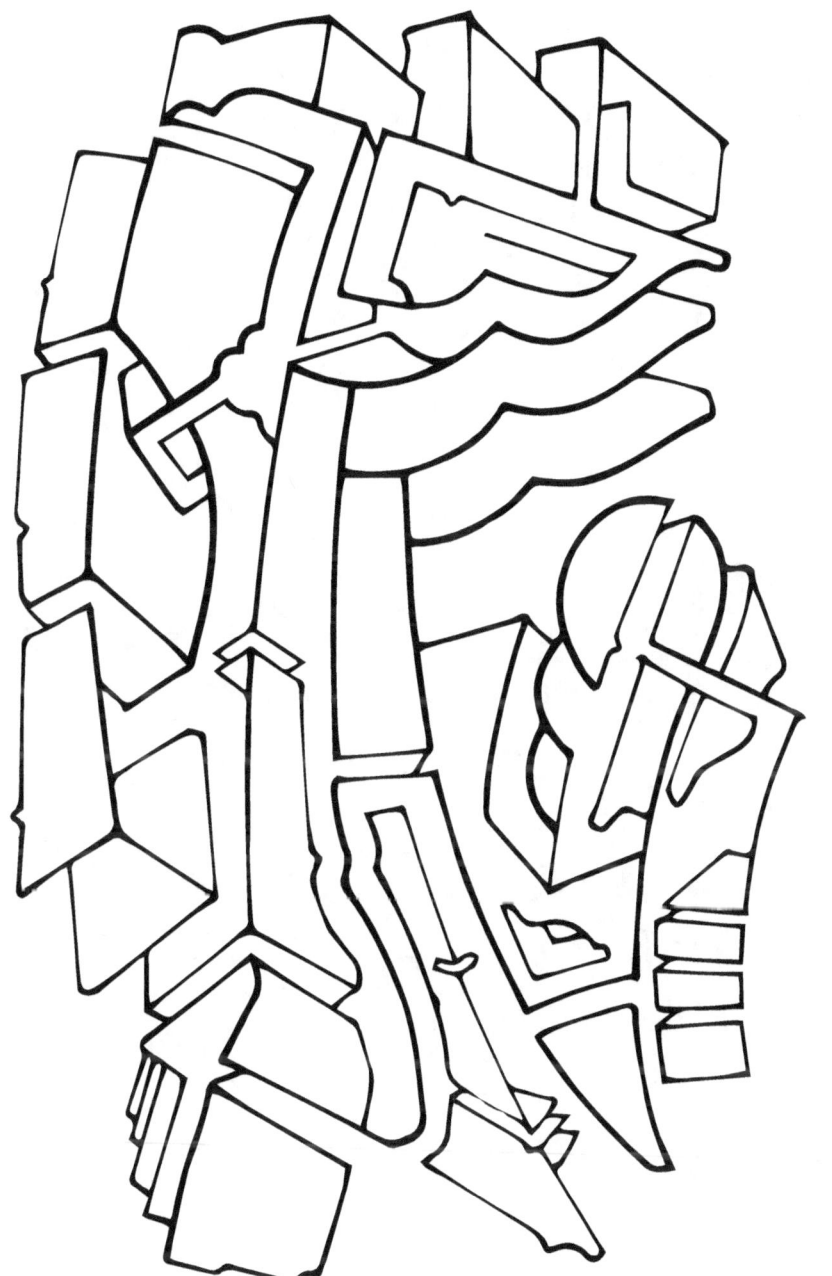

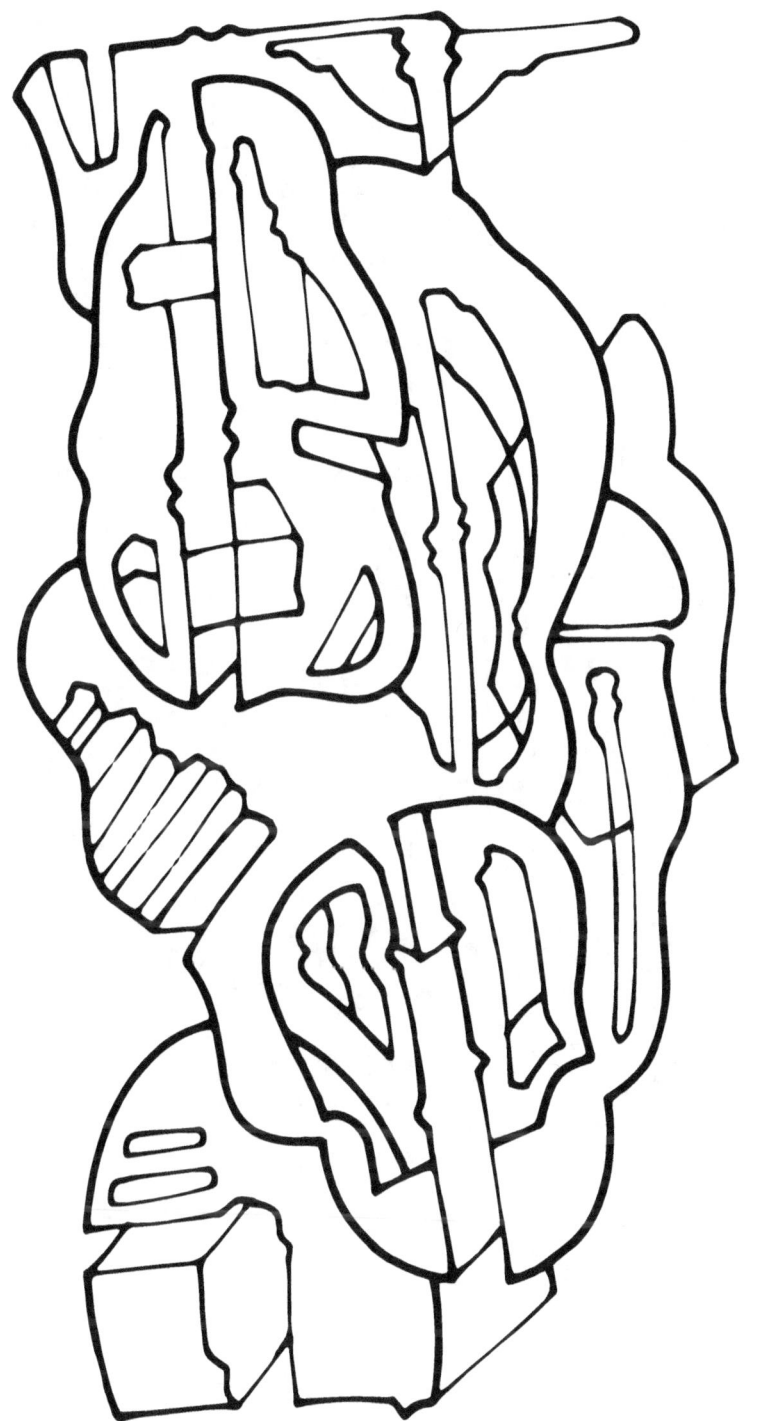

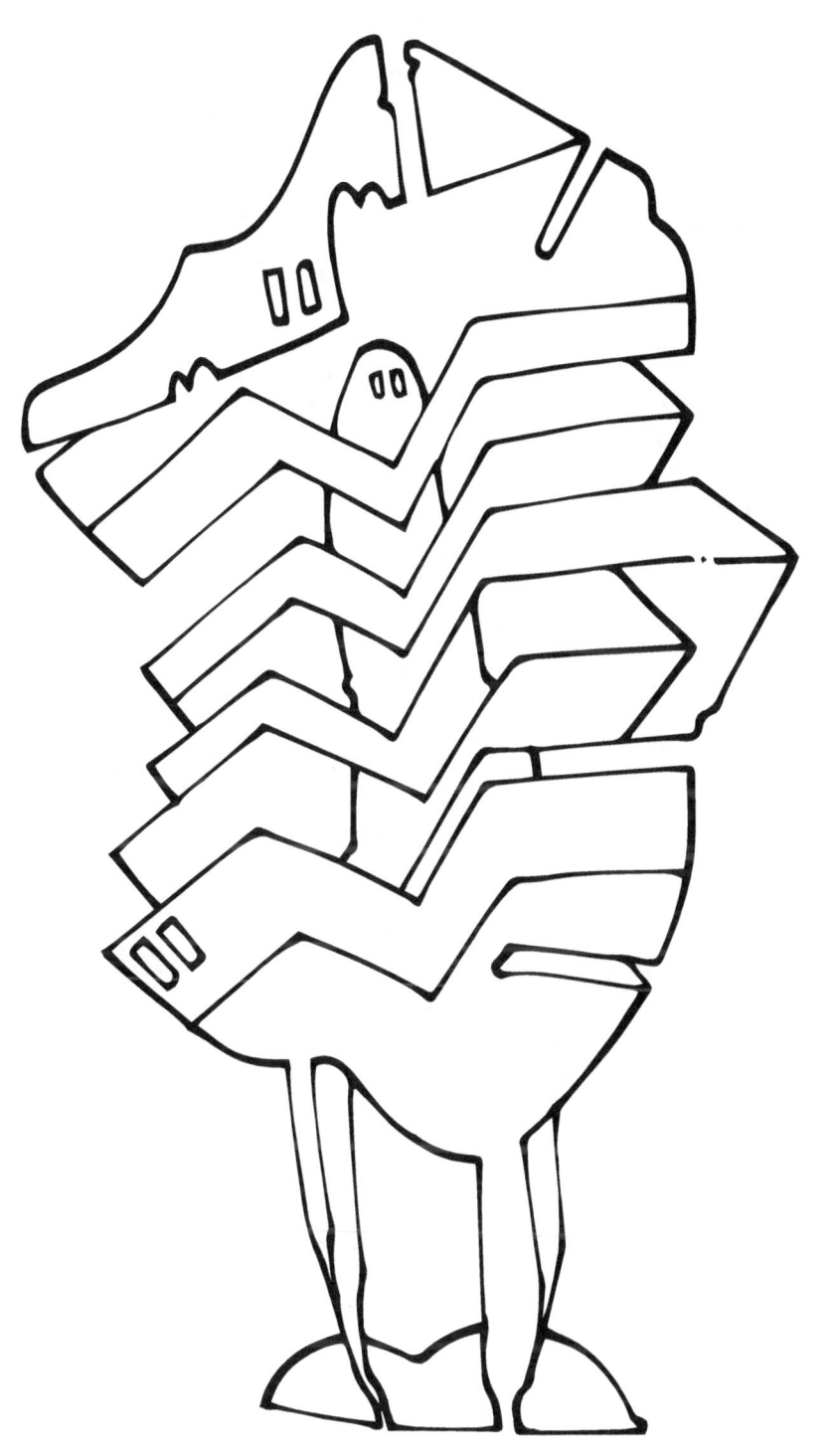

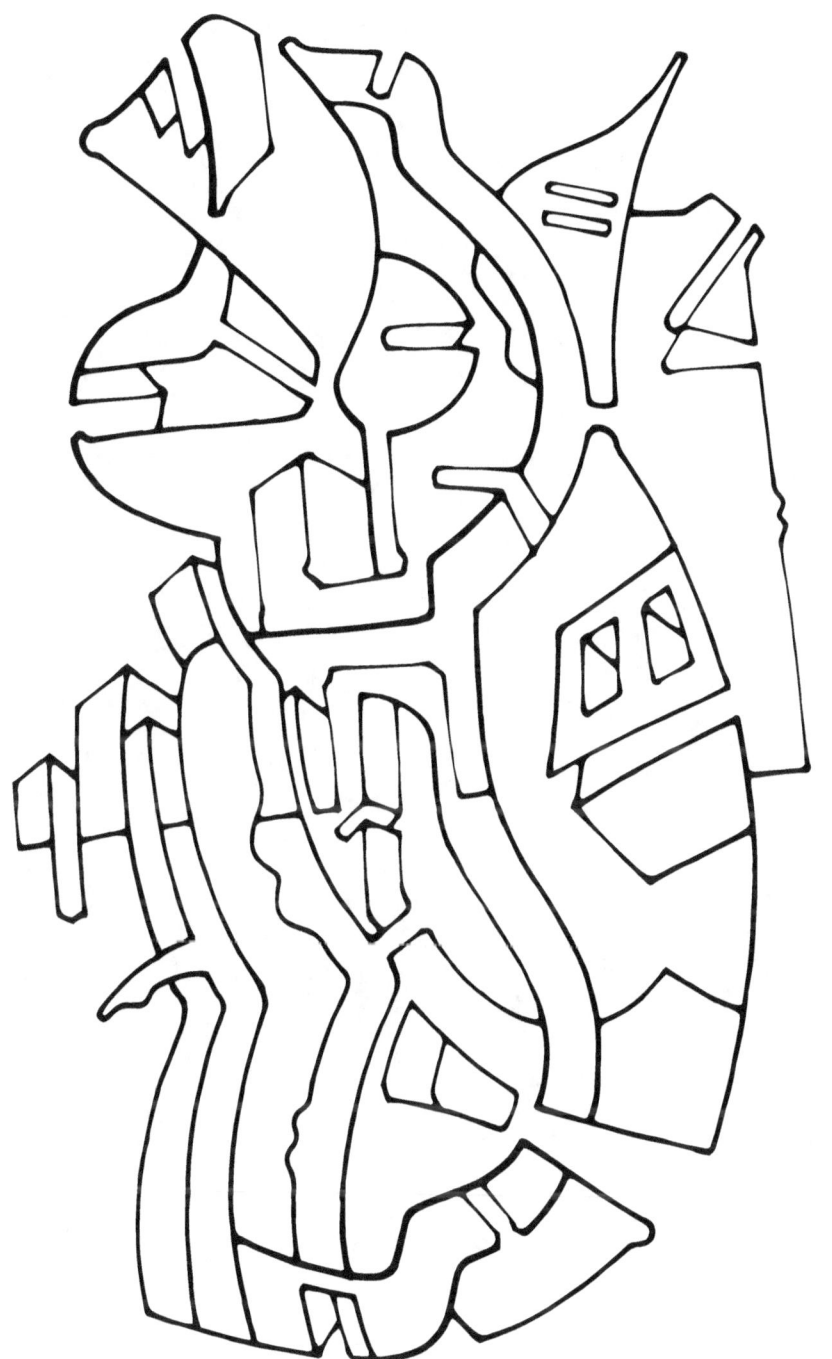

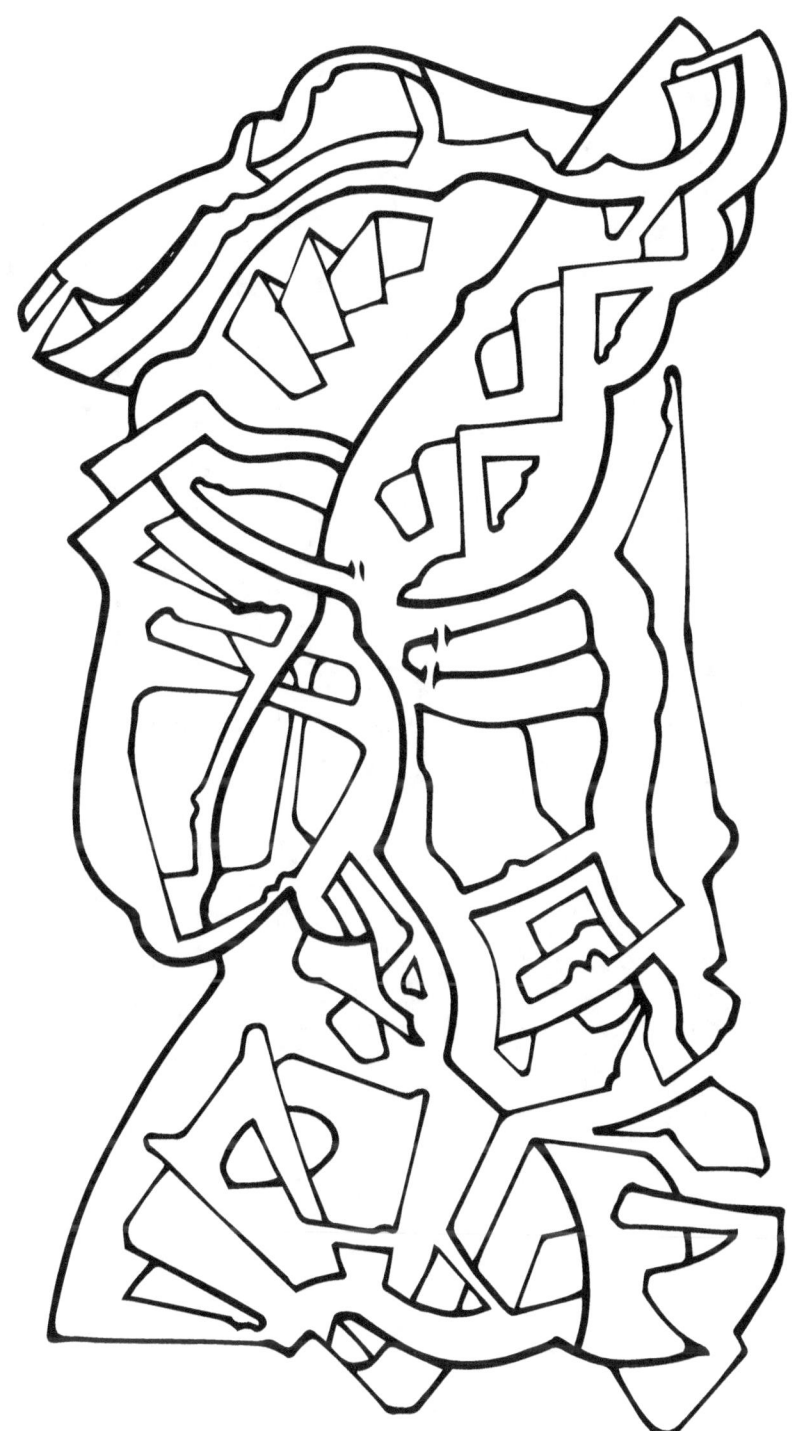

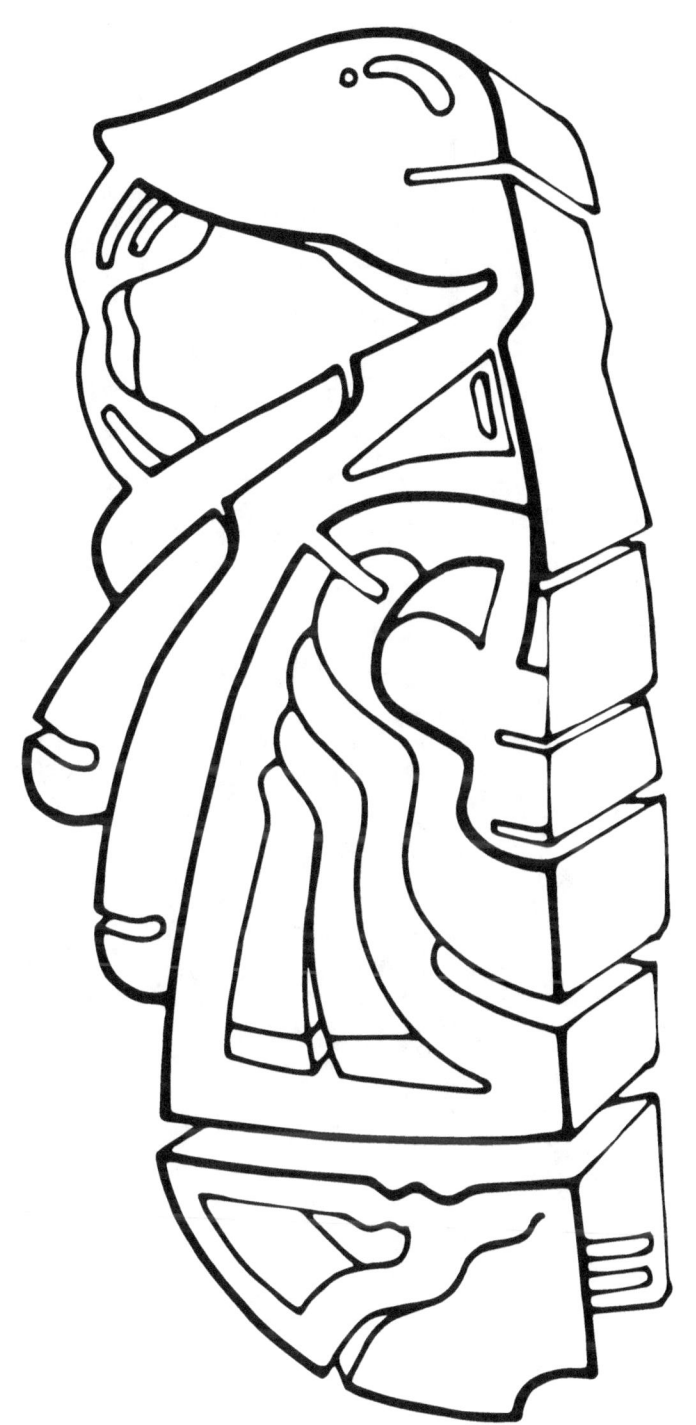

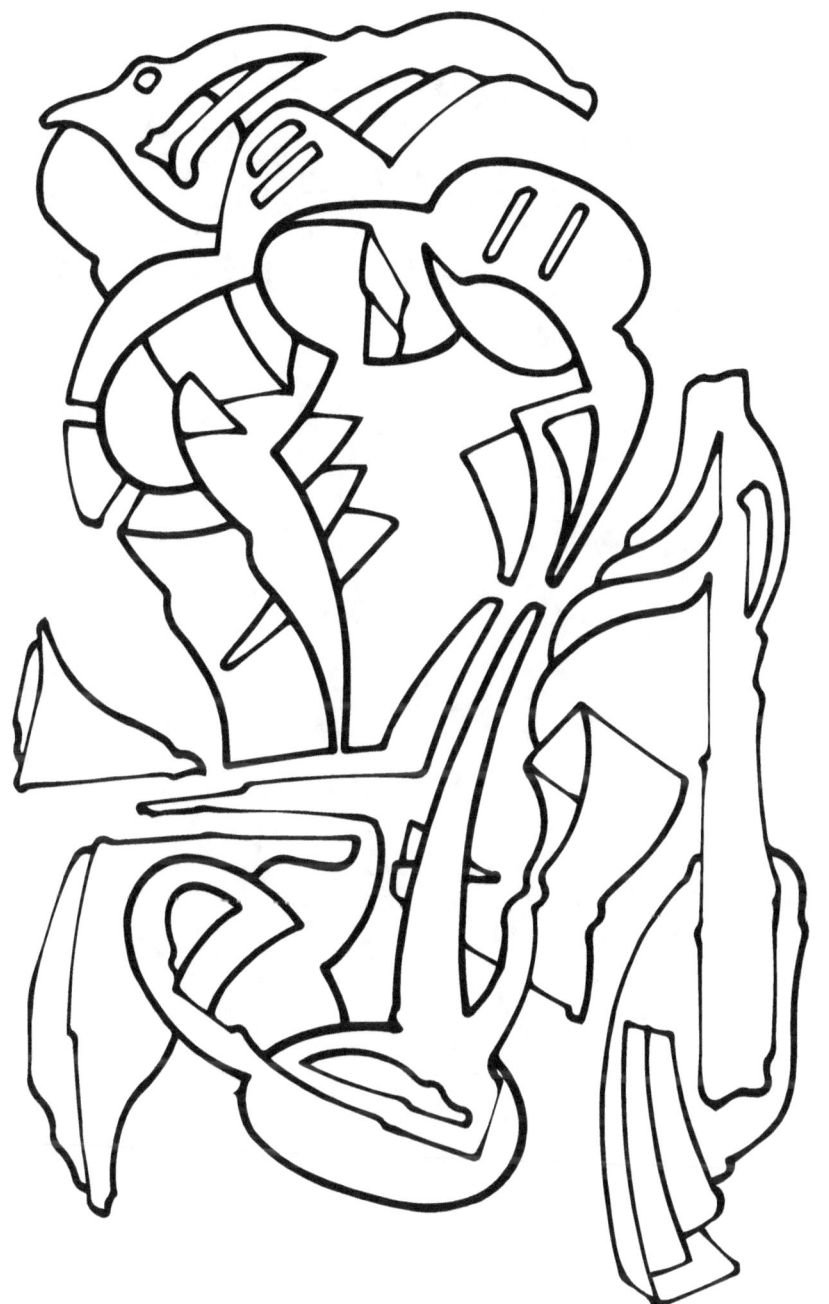

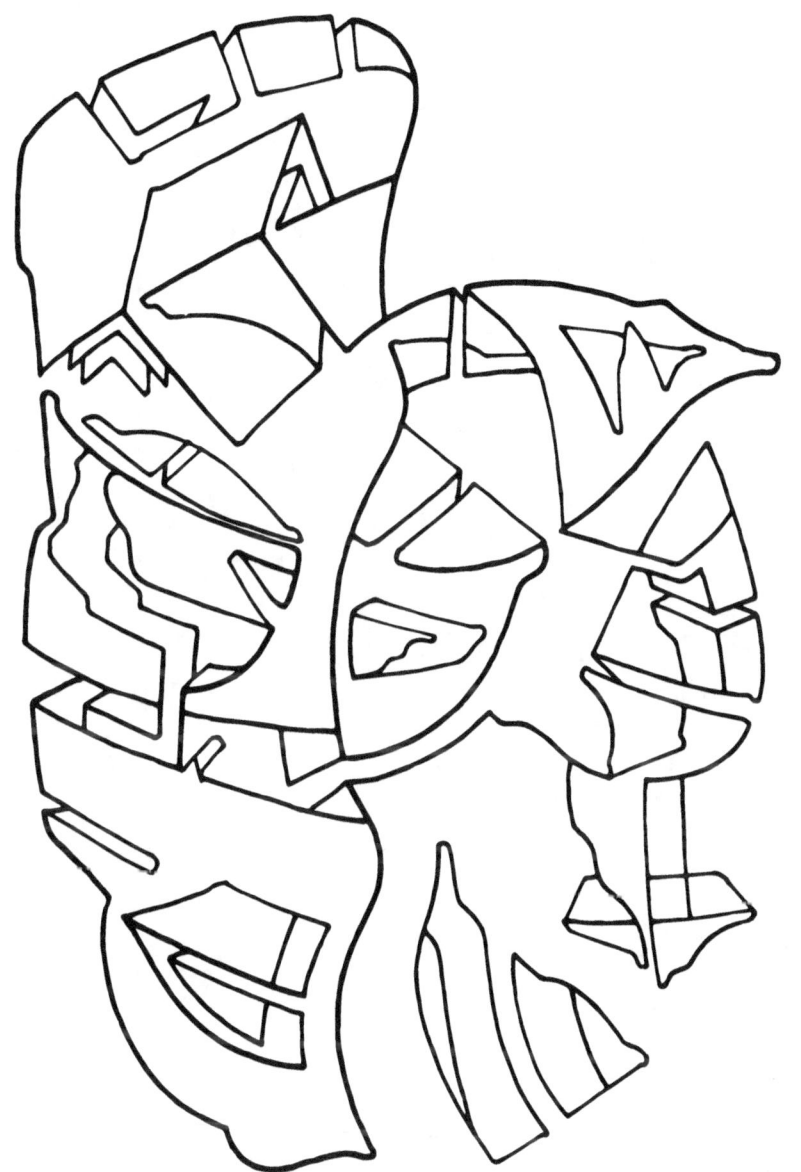

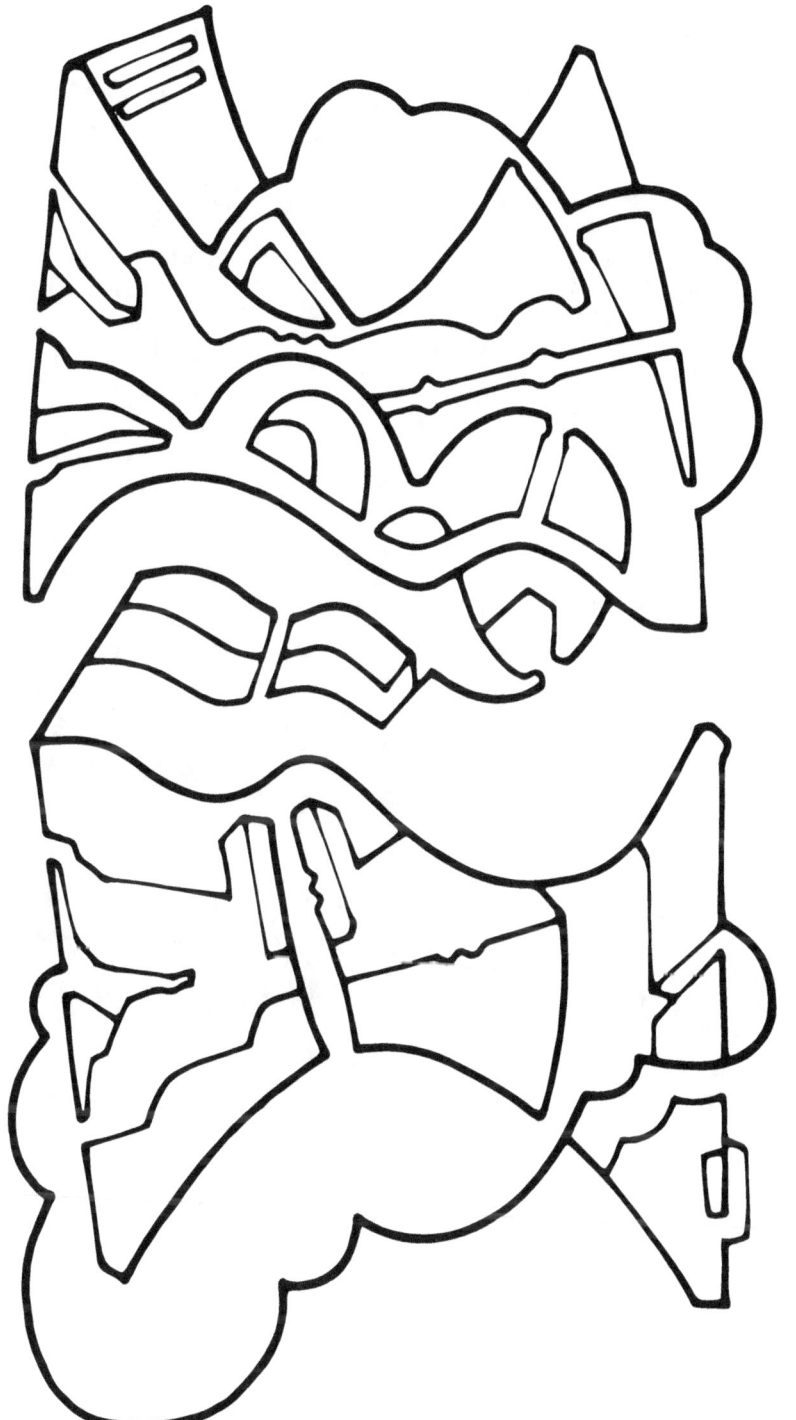

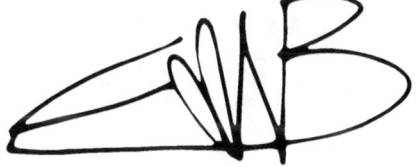

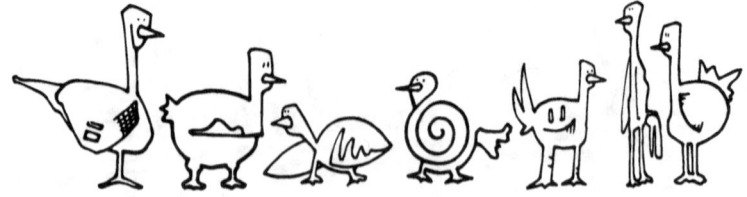

www.ingramcontent.com/pod-product-compliance
Lightning Source LLC
Chambersburg PA
CBHW071038240526
45469CB00006BD/2254